UNQUENCHABLE
THE BURNING BUSH WITHIN

Rebekah Acquah

UnQuenchable: The Burning Bush Within
Copyright © 2022 by Rebekah Acquah

Library of Congress Control Number: 2020923878
ISBN: (Paperback)   978-1639455768
     (Ebook)   978-1639455775

WRITERS'
BRANDING

Writers' Branding
1800-608-6550
www.writersbranding.com
orders@writersbranding.com

Contents

Dedication/Acknowledgements

To my husband, who trusted in God to unite us

To my mother, who believed in what God promised to her.

To my aunt who gave me a second chance to experience self-love and belief in God's plan.

To my best friends who allowed me to express my authenticity.

To every soul that will read these pages, may you receive an impact of Unquenchable Peace, Joy and Happiness.

I love you, and Thank you!.

Now Moses was tending the flock of Jethro his father-in-law, the priest of Midian, and he led the flock to the far side of the wilderness and came to Horeb, the mountain of God. There the angel of the LORD appeared to him in flames of fire from within a bush. Moses saw that though the bush was on fire it did not burn up. So Moses thought, "I will go over and see this strange sight—why the bush does not burn up." **-Exodus 3:1-3**

Author's Message

The fire within is more than what you know. Because you are unquenchable. Yes, I see that glow. One that has been there since day one, there within the day your glow hit the sun. One that is still there and second to none. Oh how it overflows..if only ... mm you know. It always shows, even when you do not recognize It. It is like a throne that has always been a throne. It. Only takes you sitting. Sitting, sitting, sitting. It's yours since birth, it's yours. What, you desire? No, it's just yours. We grow, we weep , we seek, we dive deep within. In each of you and me. It's this fire just waiting to be set free. Free! It's free. But wait , all it takes is you. Recognize! Realize. Find? No no need to look ... just recognize and realize ..how can you look for something that's never been lost .It's always been there. Born within . Yes, born within you and me. Never torn away, it's ingrained into our soul. It's ingrained with no remorse. Do you know it's ingrained? Connected to your skin that it can not be torn away.. It's just ingrained. Ingrain From your flesh it cannot be removed because it will leave a scar that will always remain. It is attached to your soul that will never let go. All it takes is for you. To recognize it. A joy that always flows. A love that always grows a smile that always shines a love that you can never leave behind. As it burns within, oh girl, boy ,man , woman , father ,mother etc.. It is Divine. I see your fire, I see your light, I see your glow, you are "Unquenchable."

Introduction - Imagine

Imagine a happiness, an unquenchable happiness that was never separated from the innermost core of your being. Now imagine recognizing that you have always had this happiness within you from the minute you were born.

We are born ultimately happy, but through our life journeys, offensive emotions overtake us as we take in everything from our experiences. Most of us lose our true happiness, that pure happiness that birth gives us. We lose that peacefulness of not knowing certain things or feeling certain negative emotions as a child, and that freedom of expression; the freedom of saying what you mean and how you feel. I truly believe that every human being that grows into adulthood goes through this, and that is okay. As a part of life, we live with our everyday stressors; and dilemmas, family, friends, and our experiences make us who we are and that is why finding our "unquenchable happy" as adults is important. Before doing so we must understand our story, and we need to figure out what changed from when we were children besides the obvious of biological growth. A happiness that derives from within and is determined to stay needs exploration. Imagine a joy that remains no matter what people say or do, or no matter what you come across, this joy remains and never dims nor fades. It is possible to be "happy" and to live as adults with that same freedom from that same peace, as when we first were born.

From college days, my classmates, college peers, friends, and people in general, young and old ask me what makes me so happy. What motivates me to see the good in someone right from the get go? Why am I so optimistic? A stranger whom I haven't really considered as a friend just yet would typically want advice from me, and will want to call me a friend and ask me for favors. Some say that they see a glow in me, while others can't really figure me out, but they find comfort in approaching me with their life situations.

To answer those lingering questions, I believe that what they may see is the glow of an individual who has a story, one which is meaningful, one that without it this individual wouldn't have such a glow. We all have stories and we all go through journeys of highs and lows, therefore no one can judge another person by their journey. Whether you believe your journey was tougher or more painful than others, it is not our job to enforce the understanding of the pain we've been through on those around us. The same thing goes for those who have been fortunate to go through a less painful story; it is not our duty to suppress our privileged lives, and meanwhile, we also have the responsibility of being grateful and not boastful. So I express happiness in my life because my journey has brought me to a place of gratefulness. It may not have been one which I would have initially chosen for myself, and it is not less nor more painful than others around me. I cannot compare my cross that I was given to that of others, but I am simply grateful that I was given a cross to carry in the first place because my cross is a representation and a reflection of what Jesus (my Higher Power) had to go through to set me free and allow me to share this joy with others. Because of my story, I recognize the fire within. So I walk with a smile, and although inside I may be a bit down and some days are not as easy, yet the joy burns within with an optimism that allows me to see past my past and be present in my present, because the features of my future are aligned with God.

As you dive into my journey, it is not for you to feel pity towards my story. It is geared towards a light of whether we are privileged to have a life of little hardship, or blessed to have a past of hardship. Each person still carries their own cross that they bear and holds an opportunity for their unquenchable happiness. Therefore, it is up to us to not be judgmental towards each other, but instead share a smile and bring optimism into our daily lives. Each of us may be the one example another individual needs to also GLOW (Give Love and Optimism to the World).

Chapter 1 - Quenched

There is a connection to the old, the young, the rich, the poor, the mentally ill, the arrogant, the happy, the Christians, the Muslims, the spiritualist, the politicians, the homemakers, the strong, the weak, the timid, the loud, the emotional, the humble, the angry, the confused, the I-know-who-I-am's, the frightened, the rude, the ghetto, the not-so ghetto, the African, the Spanish, the American—you and me.

What makes me so brave to believe that I am just like you? Out of the millions of people in this world you probably have never met me, and if you have, you probably do not know much about me, and I probably do not know you or know much about you either. What I do know is that we have something similar; there is a connection. You may not believe it, but you will soon understand what I mean. There is a quote that gets us started with knowing each other and our similarities that I truly believe in. As Paulo Coelho stated, "If you are brave to say goodbye, the Universe will reward you with a new hello." I am pretty sure that you, reading this memoir, have sometime in your life said goodbye to a loved one, perhaps a family member, a best friend, a pet, or a significant other. In this case we are already on the path of knowing each other. Let me take you to the year of 1992 in West Africa, Liberia, where my glow began.

* * * * * *

In this chapter we follow the happenings before Gloria Mansa was born. Follow as she watches her parents in love and her birth country in shambles and dismay as her life begins.

West Africa, Liberia, 1992: shooting, killing, shouting, famine, and destruction. Can a child survive in a place like this, where most young boys are given a gun to shoot their friends, family, and innocent citizens? It's a place where children are no longer looked upon as children but as potential killers, where parents and families have to leave each other behind to die or stay together and watch each other get killed before their eyes. This is not a place to give birth now, Momma. Not now. Not in the condition of this country. But Momma had no choice, did she? Momma was only fourteen, and Papa was twenty-four. Momma claimed that she was in love, that she needed Papa while ignoring the fact that he was her teacher, her babysitter, and how young she was at the time. She ignored how thin and fragile her bones were compared to his. But Papa, why couldn't you see that Momma was not ready? Each night Momma and Papa snuck out and did things that no one knew about, undressing each other as he penetrated her body. There was love in their eyes, more from Momma than Papa though. They looked happy, but it was not up to them. It had been three years since they were sneaking around, and finally, something happened.

Momma was vomiting, and she was crying. Who was she going to tell? She had no one but her only cousin, Omo. She couldn't tell Omo though. He was the one who asked Papa to watch Momma as he traveled. Omo would be devastated and ashamed of Momma and Papa. Oh, Momma, you should have known it would come to this. Momma, stop vomiting. Please make it go away. Do all you can to make it go away.

"Oh no!" she cried out.

I watched Momma run to Omo to tell him the news. Omo was so furious. He was angry and confused all at once.

"Who did this?" he asked angrily.

After Momma gave a frightened answer, Omo stormed out. He must be going to Papa's house.

"Where is he? Where is he? Where is the rapist? Where is the ingrate? Where is the backstabber? Where is he?"

Unfortunately, Papa was not home. He was at work, teaching at the school. So Omo left Papa's house. On his way, Momma followed in tears. At the school Momma saw Papa and she ran to him. Oh, Momma, why are you running to him? He's at work and you are supposed to be his student. Omo was very angry but managed to keep the little respect he had left for Papa. He pulled Papa away from his class and asked him questions that I could not understand; he was speaking fast. Papa was just standing there holding Momma. I'm guessing that they were in love, or was he just feeling sorry for himself? Everyone was watching, all of Papa's students and administrators. What would happen to Papa if this controversy came out in the open? Papa must have thought about that when he and Momma first met. They took a long time to discuss this—well, Omo was doing all the talking. Papa went on his knees! I got closer to hear what he was saying.

"I'm sorry, Omo. I'm sorry." Papa cried to Omo, but Omo walked away.

He was leaving Momma behind with Papa. Momma started running behind Omo as he walked faster. She caught up to him, and they both walked to the house.

For the entire day Momma and Omo did not talk to each other. Momma continued crying throughout the day, and Omo ignored her. The silence between them went on for a week and a half, and Momma's tears never stopped. She was already a thin little teenager at five foot two. She lost weight, and she looked so malnourished.

Four weeks passed. Momma and Papa did not see each other during that time. *Papa, why can't you come and see Momma in the condition that she is in?* I wondered. I had so many questions running through my mind; some will be answered in due time. Despite what Momma placed herself in, Omo loved Momma unconditionally, and he couldn't see her in this condition and leave her to suffer, so Omo took Momma and made her bread and tea. I watched them talk and smile for the first time in four weeks. Suddenly, amidst the joy, we heard several gunshots and screaming far in the distance. Although the war was past its peak and was ending, every now and then something happened to remind the people of Liberia that it was not fully over. Momma jumped up and ran under a table when she heard gunshots. Omo laughed and said, "It's okay, Beatrice, the gunshots are not nearby. They're far away."

She waited until she stopped hearing gunshots before she came out from under the table. Omo was one of the few family members that Momma still had. They were very close, and Omo thought of Momma as his little niece instead of his cousin. Things were looking positive again. Momma was happy, Omo was happy, and, besides the fact that the country was in famine and destruction, being happy internally at this point was a big plus.

Wait, I think I spoke too soon. It is five in the morning and Momma is leaving the house. She walked silently out the door without waking Omo. She ran toward the road. Her flip flops were ruined so she could not run fast. She slowed down and started walking. Suddenly she stopped. I remember this road; this is the same road that Omo and Momma walked on the way to Papa's school. *No, no, Momma, not again!* Before I could finish my thought, I saw a man walking up to Momma. They met and it was no one but Papa. Papa hugged Momma tight, and she had the biggest smile on her face. She put her hand down her dress and took out a plastic bag. She opened it and gave Papa bread, sardines, and water. Papa really enjoyed himself. He must be really hungry because he swallowed the bread without chewing it. Papa ate every bit of it, and Momma watched him with awe as she laughed. She looked happy. She watched him until he started laughing. He looked at her closely. He drew closer to her and touched her face; he looked into her eyes and placed his hands on her bosom. She kissed him, and he couldn't control himself, so he plunged her on the ground and made love to her. Hadn't they learned their lesson from Omo's rage and anger? Plus, this is not for my eyes; it's rather haunting.

"Beatrice! Beatrice! Beatrice! Where are you?"

Uh oh, Omo is here looking for Momma. She got up from the ground and Papa leapt up as well. They both ran the other direction. Papa looked so scared, and he ran faster than Momma. Momma was trying to keep up in her condition. Omo's voice gradually disappeared. They slowed down to catch their breath. She walked up to Papa, breathless, and fell into his arms, which caught him off guard. He caught her automatically as she nearly hit her head on the ground.

"Beatrice, Beatrice, Beatrice, Beatrice, wake up. Wake up, Beatrice!" said Papa.

But she only murmured unclear words to him. He tapped her face and felt her neck.

"Beatrice, wake up! Don't do this to me now, Beatrice."

She murmured unclear words continuously. He looked even more afraid than he was a few moments ago before while running away from Omo.

"Oh, Jesus, help me. Beatrice, please wake up."

With little response from Momma, Papa put Momma on his back. He started walking while talking to himself. He talked to Momma again, pleading with her to stay awake and saying that he was almost there.

"The sun is out really early today; it's so hot," Papa said to himself.

At least forty-five minutes passed and Papa was still walking. At this point Momma was not uttering a single word. Papa abruptly stopped by what looked like a store, and he laid her on the ground. She shook a little. What was happening to her? Papa, please help Momma. Papa came out of the store with what looked like a water bottle in his hands. He poured a lot on Momma's entire body from head to toe. Papa looked so nervous and even more scared.

"Beatrice, Beatrice can you hear me?" he asked. She was murmuring unclear words again. That was better than her not saying anything at all. Papa picked up Momma, and he started walking again. It was probably past noon, and Momma and Papa had been together since morning. Omo was probably worried about Momma or maybe he knew where she was, I mean he should have had an idea. If he did not, then he would not have tried to follow her on the same road to Papa's school.

Papa stopped again, this time at a blue little house with clothing lines. There was something in a pot on a fire in front of the house.

"Ma, Momma, Ma ooh where y'all eh?" Papa yelled.

An older lady with a lapa cloth wrapped around her waist and a blouse, with slippers on and a head tie ran out the house.

"What happened, David, why are you yelling my name?" the older lady asked Papa.

Papa grabbed the older lady and placed Momma in her hands.

"Please help me Momma, this is Beatrice, Omo's cousin. She's pregnant and she fainted and now I can't wake her up. Please Momma help her," Papa said. I figured that she must be Papa's Mom because he kept calling her Momma and she looked older than him. She took Momma into the little blue house and placed another pot on the fire in front of the house with water in it. I watched her put things in the water, but I am not sure what they were. While Papa and his Momma waited for the water to get warm, his Momma turned to him, and looked at him without saying anything.

"I know Momma what you are thinking, and yes it's mine, but please make sure she's okay before we discuss this issue."

About ten minutes passed. Papa's Momma walked back into the little blue house and brought out a bucket, poured the water into the bucket and Papa and her walked into the blue house. What is she doing with Momma? I silently asked myself as I watched. She lifted Momma. She took off all of Momma's clothes - even her underwear. She told Papa to leave the room, so he walked away. She grabbed a cloth and it looked like she was bathing Momma, she washed Momma, every part of her. She rubbed stuff on her body and dressed her in different clothes. I wanted to shout so loud, "Momma is awake Papa, Momma is awake!" but I couldn't. She looked better than she ever did. Whatever was in that pot worked a miracle. Momma and Papa's Momma walked outside to Papa, and she handed Momma back to Papa and said, "Take her back to where you took her from and stay away from her before she gets you into trouble or you get yourself fired from your school job."

Papa to his Momma: "But Ma she's pregnant with your grandchild. If I take her back to Omo he's going to report me to the school, and I will lose my job. Please Momma, let Beatrice stay here with you and Olu. She knows how to cook, clean and she can help you around the house." They went back and forth while Momma stood there.

Papa's Momma: (in Liberian English) "What made you think I need help, and what made you go and follow this little baby to get her pregnant David? You embarrass yourself amongst all your crowd of men, you don't know how to keep your thing between your legs to yourself."

Papa: "Momma it's already done. Momma. Madia is pregnant as well, so I need to go take care of her. I'm going Momma, I'm going."

Papa's Momma: "Oooooh David, David, ooh you will kill me, two pregnancies how do you do it? (Then, she turned to Momma with a scary look.) You dry stick you like man too much, went and follow my son, now you think you part of us … no no small girl like you my son will not marry you not when I'm alive and breathing, over my dead body."

Momma was tearing up. I can't believe Papa's Momma was this mean to Momma. Papa turned to Momma and said, "Beatrice, please stay with my Ma and Olu until I come back. I will be back in a couple weeks, I promise. Don't worry, they will take good care of you and please help them out around the house."

Momma agreed with Papa. She must have loved him so much that she had no choice but to agree. Papa left and Momma moved to run behind him, but Papa's Momma grabbed onto her so fast.

Momma started crying again. I stayed with Momma to have an understanding of her side. Papa's Momma left Momma outside crying. Momma cried for hours, and then suddenly a young girl approached Momma with a big bowl she was carrying over her head. She saw Momma crying and approached her. She looked like she was in her late teens or early twenties. She was very tall and skinny with a nice hourglass shape. Her skin was almost like Momma's, but she was lighter than Momma and her hair was long. You couldn't tell exactly how long her hair was because it was braided in cornrows. She removed the bowl from her head quickly and asked Momma why she was crying. Momma said nothing while she continued to cry, she wiped Momma's eyes and held her.

"Beatrice, stop crying. Stop crying Beatrice. Whatever you're crying for, it's going to go away." She must know Momma because she said her name, and Momma responded to her. "Olu this one won't go away. Olu it can't. David na do it again Olu."

"What David na do again, what are you talking about?" the girl asked Momma. Momma called her Olu, and I figured this is the same Olu that Papa was talking about earlier with his Momma.

Momma told Olu: "Beatrice pregnant me and Madia at the same time and left me here to go take care of Madia. Omo probably thinks I ran away, and he went to David school to look for me. David Momma just cussed me and left me outside. Olu, this one can't go away. Olu, help me; I think I want to die."

Olu to Momma: "No one is dying here today. Beatrice you will be fine, now just stop crying and help me cook. Let's wait for David, he will come back soon okay; don't worry."

Olu helped Momma get up off the ground. Momma wiped her face with her clothes and followed Olu in the house. Olu headed to the kitchen area as Momma followed immediately behind. Olu grabbed a pot and told Momma to look in a box that's sitting on the floor and get the plantains. Momma did what Olu instructed her to do, and after grabbing everything they needed, they went outside and started to cut up the meats, the plantains and the greens that Olu took from inside. I watched closely. The natural way in which the meal was being prepared was fascinating to watch. I was so focused on the preparation of the food that I forgot to pay attention to what Momma was saying to Olu. I diverted my attention back to them.

Momma asked Olu: "Olu did you know that Madia is pregnant with David's child?"

Olu: "Yes, Beatrice, I know. David brings Madia here to the house often and Ma likes Madia, she said that she's David's age and will make David stop being gruna, passing around with different women everywhere in this town knowing full well that he is a teacher. That's why she was furious when he brought you here today to tell her you're pregnant by him."

Momma: "So why did David put me in this, lie to me and said he loves me, I'm the only one? Now he impregnated me and left to go to his other woman?"

Olu: "Well Beatrice, my dear, David didn't put you in this alone ooh. You like David and I know he's way older than you but you like David, so right now all you can do is leave David business. Since you know now that he has another woman pregnant, just stay here small, take care of yourself, help around small and give birth to your baby. If David comes back then he comes back, but if not, give God the glory and take care of your child. Some men are not good and even though David is my uncle, when it comes to woman business, he is a dog, not good."

After Olu mentioned Papa being her Uncle It was a shocker, as she looked like she was around Papa's age. That meant Papa must have a sister, I thought to myself.

Momma to Olu: "Okay Olu I hear you ... don't worry, I will finish cooking the food. You and the Olma can jes rest for the day."

Olu asked Momma if she was sure, and after Momma said yes, Olu stayed with Momma and watched her finish making the food. Papa's Momma came outside the house and looked at what Momma was doing. She gave Momma a dirty look, hissed her teeth and went on her way saying to Olu that she was going to the market.

Olu told Momma: "Do not worry about the Olma (Papa's Momma). She is just a mother who doesn't want her son to get in trouble for impregnating one of his students and remember that Omo is one of David's good friends and you are Omo's relative. This situation now might ruin their friendship, and it probably already has."

Momma did not reply to Olu; instead, she continued preparing the food. The sun was still out and Momma was almost done with cooking, she grabbed one of the big bowls they brought outside and poured the greens soup in the big bowl, and then took the little bowls and gave them to Olu to share. Olu shared the soup and left a small amount in the big bowl. Then she took the rice and shared it into the smaller bowls. She poured the leftovers into the bigger bowl with a small amount of soup. As Olu took the shared food into the house, Momma started taking the pots in the back. I watched her as she put the pots on the ground, and then she went inside the house for water to wash the pots outside. As she did so, a man came and stood over her and watched her until she finished with the pots.

He asked her: "Beatrice, what are you doing here?"

Momma replied: "Hello."

He asked again: "I said what are you doing here, washing pots?"

Momma replied: "I just finished cooking y'all food in the house and now I'm washing the pots that I used."

He said: "So who told you to come here again and now you're telling me you just cook food for us. Where's David? Why are you here again?"

Momma replied: David is not here. He brought me here to stay. I don't feel like talking plenty so please go ask Olu and she will tell you why I'm here. Just let me be, please."

He stood there for a few seconds and screamed Olu's name several times. Olu came out and he asked Olu the same questions he asked Momma. Olu filled him in on what went on through the day and why Momma was there. The next thing I know, he started grabbing Momma, telling her to leave, and that she didn't belong there, and she was too skinny and dry for his brother David. He continued with his outrage on Momma as Olu pulled her away. The last words that came out of his mouth were very heartbreaking. He said to Momma as Olu pulled her away, " David will never marry you, and you and that bastard child do not belong here."

The tears that poured down Momma's face showed how terrible she felt about what he said. As I watched, I couldn't believe how he was treating Momma and she was taking it all. I hoped that this was the worst that it could get, but if only that was true. Before I could even finish my thought something happened that started a new discovery.

Chapter 2 - Not Alone

Momma stayed with Papa's family for several months, and although she was sheltered under their roof, it was a difficult condition for a malnourished pregnant teenager. The Liberian Civil War was still going on, which was one of Africa's bloodiest, and claimed the lives of more than 200,000 Liberians and further displaced a million others into refugee camps in neighboring countries. This was the time of the second civil war. In combination with one more war in later years, Liberia endured three wars within 14 years, from 1988-2003.1

Chapter 3 - A Child Is Born

Today is November 29.

As Momma awakens, her stomach was hurting and the pain gradually exudes in intensity. She didn't tell anybody. She went into the bathroom, it looked as though she was menstruating but it was more so water pouring down her legs.

She rushed to a cousin of the family and told her, "It looks like I'm seeing my period but with lots of water." The woman said, "You are in labor pain dear." They went and called Olu, and Olu brought along with her another family member they called Aunty Musu, She looked much older than Olu. They took Momma to a clinic on Madonna Street. The doctor was nowhere to be found so they had to take a car to bypass the war conditions that were happening in the country. They arrived at Catholic Hospital. Being new there and since it was during the war and Momma looked so young, the Doctor asked Aunty Musu to Sign for Momma as being responsible for her before he could operate on her to deliver the baby. Everybody was scared to sign. They knew that the pregnancy was risky after the Doctor told Momma that the child may come out blind if she didn't take a certain medication he gave her during the pregnancy. Olu took the pen and signed. Bombing surrounded them. The doctor asked Momma where the father of the child was. She said, "He abandoned me when I was four months pregnant; I don't know where he is."

They told her they would give her stitches without anesthetic, so they wanted her to understand she was going to feel extreme pain. It was her first time having a baby, they cut her vagina without anesthetics to allow the baby to come out. At 8pm a beautiful baby girl was born. They stitched her up after giving birth as promised without anesthetic. Momma remained at the hospital for one night; there was no one to take care of Momma or the baby. Olu had to go back and forth to the hospital. Momma ended up going home with Olu. She sat in salt water each day to help heal her stitches. She did not rest as a new mother, with the pain of childbirth stitches, she still had to prepare food.

The next ordeal for the child was when Momma noticed the child's right foot was slightly crippled; the vein was out of place. This was not noticed in the hospital due to the chaos of the many patients and the condition of the war. Momma fell on her belly during her pregnancy when she was trying to escape from a helicopter of shooting men, and as a result her daughter's leg was slightly crippled. With the help of Olu, the child's leg became normal. Every day, for months, Olu stretched her leg with an African remedy and lukewarm water. As months went by, the child began to recognize her mother's touch. I, Gloria Mansa, now saw my mother and felt an ultimate bond. With the war still going on and family members separating, Momma and I ended up separated from Olu and the others. We returned to Momma's town, with whom she was more familiar.

I lived with my mom and her friend as neighbors in a compound. I attended school as any child would, and spent my free time playing with my best friend in the backyard. Whenever school was out I was happy to go home and play with her, I was now five years old.

Me: "Hi !"

Nini: "Hi Gloria, wanna go make something behind the yard?"

Me: "Yep, let's make soup. My Momma is cooking today, we can get some things from her that she's not using, but she can't see us taking it."

Nini: "Okay. I like your mom, she's really nice."

Me: "Ya me too, she doesn't beat me; I like that part best. My mom is the sweetest mother ever. She can hold me tight; she is always smiling, and sounds just like me, you can't even tell she's hurting and in pain when she's with me. She doesn't show anger or sadness, but I know as young as I am that she is hurting somehow. I mean she doesn't talk much about my Papa; maybe she feels I'm too young to understand or maybe she just wants to live in the moment with me. But what's funny to me is that I don't even ask her about him because I'm so happy with her that it doesn't cross my mind. Maybe I am too young to understand or even want to ask."

Nini: "How do you think your Papa looks?"

Me: "I see a light skinned, tall, handsome man coming to our house once In a while giving me and my friends presents; maybe he's my Papa. He's so nice and hugs me when he comes here, but he doesn't stay long."

Nini: "Maybe he goes to work for long and sleeps there."

Me: "Well maybe, I don't think so. If he is my Papa I hope he comes tomorrow for my birthday. I'm turning six, Momma said."

Nini: "That's awesome! What your Momma doing for you for your birthday?"

Me: "She said we're going to the beach. You should ask your Momma if you can come.

Nini: "Okay... ... ... um are we going to get the things from your mom now? We already have the can to put it in."

Me: "Oh yeah, let's go!!"

Nini and I went to the front of the yard, but Momma wasn't there, only the food was on the fire but everything that she usually has as leftovers was cleaned up already. I decided to ask her, and the only place I could think of her being was with my best friend's mom, so Nini and I ran happily to her place. My Momma wasn't there, so I left with her Momma and ran to my house looking for my Momma. I ran yelling, "Momma, Momma! (I threw open the room door.) Momma!!"

I found Momma but she was with a man in the room.

Momma: saying loudly, "Gloria close the door!!"

(I closed the door quickly and Momma came outside the room.)

Me: started sobbing: "I'm sorry Momma, I didn't know. I'm sorry Momma, I'm sorry."

Momma: angrily: "I told you not to slam door open without knocking, you will not go free today."

Me: crying heavily now: "I won't do it again."

I couldn't believe it. My Momma was about to beat me for the first time; she was so upset with me. She told me to get a switch (stick from the tree in the backyard). I sobbed as I went to get the stick. I guess my Nini's Momma heard the commotion and came to see what was going on. I place the stick in Momma's hand. I could see that she didn't want to beat me, but she had no choice. She had to show me discipline and to listen when she told me something. Instead Nini's Momma looked at her and took the stick from her.

She told me to show her the palm of my hand, I looked at Momma and did what Nini's Momma asked of me. Momma didn't beat me that day , Nini's Momma did. I told Momma sorry and I wouldn't do it again. I wondered why she didn't beat me.. She looked sad afterwards. Momma gave me a bath a few minutes later after her guy friend left and I slept the rest of the day. I guess Momma was cooking for her friend, but I will never know, because he left. I don't think that was my Papa either.

Momma: "Wake up Gloria, Gloria, Happy Birthday!!"

Me: "Morning Momma, it's my birthday?"

Momma: "Yes ooh, my Gloria, my daughter, it's your special day, and its President Tubman Day too, so today is a holiday in Liberia. Everyone will be celebrating your birthday because you are sooo special."

Me: "Momma, are we still going to the beach?"

Momma: "Yes, but later on."

Me: "Can my bestfriend Nini come?"

Momma: "Sure, but she will be with her Mom celebrating the holiday today, so it might be just me and you, okay?"

Me: "Okay."

It's my sixth birthday today and a holiday too. Momma and I went to the parade for the president's birthday celebration with Nini and her Momma. It was amazing there; everyone was so happy and Momma told me they were celebrating my birthday. Momma and I stayed at the celebration parade for a while until it was time to go to the beach. It was a really hot day, perfect for the beach. The beach was about an hour away from us. Momma got a taxi for us to go for my special day. When we arrived, I wondered where she took the money from to pay the taxi man.

The beach was so nice, especially with Momma. I love my Momma so much. We walked and played by the water. Momma put me on her back and swung me around. We sat down and she told me a story about the water and the sky and how special I was to her, and that God made me especially for her. Momma and I played all day on the beach, and while playing a man came over to us. I was too short to really see his face, but he had a black thing on his side while he and Momma were talking. I tapped Momma and asked her what the black thing was; she said it was a camera. The man wanted to take our picture. I told him it's your birthday today. I was even happier because I loved taking pictures with Momma. She didn't have a lot of pictures of us, so we took a lot on my birthday. After the pictures, the man sat down and watched Momma and I play in the water. I don't think he was my dad either. I didn't want Momma to cry, so I didn't ask her.

Momma said it was time to leave the beach because it was getting late, plus I was tired already. I felt like I had the best Momma in the whole world. We went home and took a bath and then Momma put me to sleep. Her friend followed us home to give our pictures to us on the way. I don't remember if he left and went home or if he slept outside afterwards. I was sleeping in Momma's arms.

I woke up the next day for school, so excited to see Nini and tell all my other friends about the beach. Momma walked me to school and I told her about my plans to tell my friends about the beach and my birthday.

She laughed and said, "I'm happy you enjoyed your birthday Gloria.".

I told her how I couldn't wait for my next birthday, as I will be turning 1,2,3,4,5,6,7!! And all my birthdays will be with my Momma.

One year and five months later ... ...

"As little children see the world as perfect and the touch of a mother as everlasting, oh how devastating it is to reconstruct their minds and install reality at such a young age." - **Rebekah Acquah**

Chapter 4 - Departure

At the innocent age of six I did not know that that would be my last full year with my mother for a very long time, and I don't think she was aware either. Our bond was inseparable and she loved me with every bone in her body, and it showed. I had the best mother in the Universe. But my next experiences made me appreciate a mother's touch even more than I ever thought in my little six year old's wildest dreams.

> "A mother's touch is more unique than two lovers who confess in giving their lives for the other. Thus, when a mother's touch departs from her child, the child's soul derails into depression in the hopes of rekindling with a mother's touch."
>
> **-Rebekah Acquah**

(Crying heavy crying and wailing, tears unstoppable) ... ."No Momma, no Momma, I don't want to go! I don't want to go Momma, Momma please don't make me leave you! Momma please don't make me go ... they're going to kill me Momma. Please, I don't want to go Momma please. ..."

I hung unto my Momma in fear that she would let me go with the people that came for me. Although I knew who they were because they were family, all I had ever known in the short six years I'd been alive was my Momma and me. Even when I go and visit my aunties in their nice beautiful houses, I knew that I would be back with my Momma soon. But this time seemed different than all the other times. Momma uttered the words that I was going to spend some time over at my aunties to visit, but in a far place. When she told me that I was going to America to spend time and I will see her soon, it felt so different; I could see in her eyes that she was unsure. She began to cry and didn't want to let me go, and I certainly was not leaving my mom in tears. I asked, "Momma am I coming back?"

She answered yes, wiped her eyes and said, "It's getting late now Gloria; they're waiting for you. Please promise me you will be a good girl and always pray."

She hugged me and everyone else in our yard came and gave me a hug. My best friend hugged me and gave me a twenty-five cent Liberian coin saying, "Use it in America to buy something."

I was still confused; I didn't know where this America everyone was talking about. I just knew that I was going to listen to Momma because she promised I would be back soon. She said I was going to visit and my Papa's people were the ones who sent for me.

Momma: "Your pa wants to see you, and because of the war, one of your aunty on your pa side sent for you to go to America with your grandma and other people. I want the best for you my daughter, and right now we are just managing. It's hard on us, so just be a good girl for Mommy and go with the people, okay? I promise we will see each other soon. Wipe your eyes ehn and don't cry, because if you cry I will cry (she smiled). I love you so much Gloria. You're my only child, my first born. God is in control. Don't forget to pray, okay?" I could see her holding the tears back, so that I wouldn't shed any more than I already was. Finding it hard to let go, afraid of leaving her … …

I hugged Momma with tears still in my eyes and said goodbye. That was the last time I felt my Momma's touch for the next 17 years.

So, I left with the people that came to get me. According to my Momma, they were my daddy's family, so that meant they were my family. Although I was only seven at the time, I was pretty smart. I could read and write and sound out words that I didn't know how to pronounce well. I figured out we were going very far away from Momma with all the different signs and things that I did not recognize. We ended up sleeping on the bus car that we were traveling on. They stopped to get food and bought me something to eat. I keep saying "they" because I honestly didn't know who "they" were, I only knew the people were my daddy's family members. So after a long trip, we finally got off the bus car and started walking. People were selling and yelling at other people on the street, saying stuff like "Kool aid, kool aid, buy some kool aid one dollar for kool aid." I love kool aid so I asked one of the guys from my dad's family if he can buy me kool aid. "Uncle can you please buy me kool aid? I'm thirsty."

I was surprised but happy he bought me red kool aid. It was so good and I started liking my dad's family. We walked until we passed the market and went to a compound where people lived. There was this one big brick building with twelve doors facing the same way, and at the time we arrived, most of the doors were open with people inside. One of the guys went to the fourth door as we got closer and went inside, we followed him. I overheard him calling someone inside in Liberian English, "Momma Momma, Grandma, Grandma where ya at?" "Momma we na bring Gloria, ooh." Suddenly a woman came outside one of the two rooms that was in the place. She was so happy, and she gave me a hug.

"Oooh Gloria finally I get to see my niece again, you dry ooh, you need to eat some food. You hungry?"

Me: "No aunty."

The woman: "Why are you acting like you momo (shy) , you don't know we are your family? This is your cousin, my son, small Gabe

25

(pointing to the younger light skinned guy, who was very thin but handsome with a low haircut) and your uncle (pointing to the older light skinned guy who looked like he was either in his late 20's or early 30's and tall). Your Grandma is in the room sleeping but when she wakes up she will be so happy to see her namesake (I was named after someone). The two Gloria's in the house now. Oh Mark, your cousin is still in school. He will be here soon. That's your Uncle's son, so he's like your brother. You see, your uncle here is your father's brother from the same Ma and Pa so you and Mark have the same blood." At this point I was listening, but my seven-year old mind kept thinking about my mom.

So I asked Aunty after she was done telling me about my cousin Mark, "Aunty, when am I going back to see my Momma?"

She replied, "Don't worry, you will see her soon, but tomorrow we're going to register you for school since you will be here for some time before yall leave to go to America okay, ehn your mom told you was going to America?" I shook my head, yes.

Aunty said, "Don't shake your head; say yes or no Aunty."

Me: "Yes Aunty."

I stayed with "Aunty" and the others for about six months. I went to school and loved it. There were times I missed my mother but I gradually got used to the place where I was. I made friends at school and my cousin Mark and I were pretty close. My grandma Gloria became a protection for Mark and me. She would call me a special name 'Doll ma" and told me it's because I was named after her and that made me special. I also was very close to my other cousin, Gabe. He was such a sweetheart and would always take time out of his day to spend with me and tell me stories. While with Aunty, a tragedy occurred and we lost Gabe to a sickness unfamiliar to everyone. I felt so much pain when I no longer saw him around. His sweet smell was still surrounding every inch of the neighborhood. His memory has lasted with me until this day. To me that was my first major loss but my second loss because my first was my mother, not knowing when I would see her again.

Chapter 5 - Departure Part 2

We entered the United States on February 21, 2001. I can still remember every feeling I had on that day. I was in a strange place, not knowing where I was or why I was there, while wondering where my mother was. How long was it going to be until I would see her again? We were picked up by a woman whom I slightly remembered seeing in photos. Later I found out this was my aunt Musu who had sent for all of us to come to this strange land called America. The skies were clear on the day she greeted us and welcomed us to the United States. She took us to this place where I later learned was an apartment. There were a total of thirteen of us, and we were all amazed because of the stories we heard about America in our homeland Liberia. It was a small apartment, and we did what we could to feel comfortable there as a family. No one really complained; we were all just happy to be together. Some people slept in the rooms and some slept on the floors with blankets and sheets. But it would not be too long before aunt Musu would make provision for all of us to move into a bigger home.

Months passed and we were slowly getting into the American groove of things, but we were not quite there yet. As for me, I would take rice and torborgee (an African dish) to school for lunch and all the kids would look at me weirdly. With no hesitation I would eat it all in front of them saying, "My friends y 'all missing out."

At age nine, Aunt Musu moved us into a nicer house with 3 bedrooms, plus an attic which was made into another room, a basement, a big kitchen, living room, dining room and a nice backyard. Now we were feeling what the real America felt like, or so some of us thought. Meanwhile the sweetness of America was slowly but surely about to turn sour in our mouths. At first things were going well. We all felt like a nice big family. The older boys began working and the younger kids went to school and helped with the house chores. Then, things gradually shifted. Aunty Musu who we all were told to call "Mommy" became very tough. There was little to no freedom in the home and everyone, including her husband, was on their tippy-toes. After two and a half years of being in the house the older boys started leaving the home. Some were kicked out, and others decided to leave. It went from ten people living in the home to six people. I was hoping that there weren't any more changes but one more change occurred, which left me all alone in a big four bedroom home with Aunty Musu. Aunty Musu and her husband separated, and the remaining two children went with him. Due to the fact of me being my dad's child I had no option of leaving with them, since Aunty Musu was my father's sister. After everyone left, and the house became very lonesome, strange and scary all at the same time. Meanwhile those immediate feelings were some of the best that I would probably remember, after what was to happen next.

Chapter 6 - Runaway Child

Then it all began!!

Statistics and research says running away from home once decreases the likelihood that a youth will graduate from high school by 10% (Aratani & Cooper). Running away from home multiple times decreases the likelihood of completing high school by 18% (Aratani & Cooper). 47% of runaway/homeless youth indicated that conflict between them and their parent or guardian was a major problem (Westat, Inc).

Although these statistics may render some truths, from ages 9 to 14 I was heading towards being amongst that 47 percent, that 18% and amongst the 10%. I ran away at least twice every two months, making it sixty times within four years. Was I just a spoiled little girl who was afraid of discipline? Was I just being a teenager who was consumed by rebellious intentions? Or perhaps I, being African, was culturally disobedient? Maybe I was just looking for trouble and wanted to get my parental guardian in trouble? The reasons behind my leaving my house in the morning and not returning or leaving randomly during the day for hours before being found and returned home, at the time may have been irrelevant or unknown to myself. Meanwhile, imagine being in a four sided box with only one hole in it that gives you air. Having been placed in this box, suddenly, poisonous fumes are placed in the box, roaches are placed in the box, pins are now placed in the box hurting your skin, and suddenly a vacuum of dust is blown in the box. Then enters a little black snake that is portrayed as your best friend because you've been in the box for so long, indulging in the fumes, the dust, the poison, which all are slowly killing you, starting from your brain, and entering your organs, you see the snake as a pet. That's your best friend, and then suddenly the snake bites you. You realize it is also poisonous, its venom has already begun its effect in your internal organs; you're on your few last breaths but suddenly you see the one hole that's been there all this time that may be a chance of peace for a moment; a fresh air break. So, you take the chance. Despite all the destruction that has already been done, you decide to leave the box through that tiny hole and all you could get through the hole was your head, because the rest of your body couldn't fit. The rest of you have already been too far in the process of fading. You tried sixty times because even for that moment of just your head being able to escape for air, it keeps you going until someone frees you from that box.

Now this box in which I speak about was my experience from 9-14 years old. I was mentally, physically, and emotionally drained. The box represented the four walls of the home. After everyone left the home it was just me and my aunt Musu. At first it wasn't so bad. Although it was scary being in a big house by myself most of the time, it wasn't that bad. Gradually it became that box I described. The beatings wouldn't stop. They went from once every two weeks to once a week, to twice a week, then three to four times a week into three to four times a day when she was around. I couldn't understand the things I did wrong, and I didn't know the difference because the beatings came whether I did wrong or right. It was too much to keep up. I was afraid to watch TV in the living room at a certain time both during the day and at night. Once the front door would begin to open, my heart would start pounding. My stomach would start churning, and a sense of nervousness would overtake my tiny body. I was prepared for anything at that moment. At times once the door rang or I heard the sound of a key being inserted, I would run upstairs quickly and pretend to be sleeping. But that did not stop the beatings or the words from coming that moment, mostly at night.

As my room door opened, and the light flickered on, I would hear, "Gloria, why is the tub not clean?"

"I cleaned it Mommy, I made sure I did."

"You lying. Come here. Does this look clean to you?" I dare not say a word at this point. Silence; complete silence. It was 12:00am, but she would insist:

"Come on scrub this tub right now. I'm coming for you, just wait for me."

I already knew the next course of this night, but I wasn't sure if it would be her hands, the hanger, the shoe, the belt or anything she could find. That part was usually a mystery. But this time it was the high heel shoes. As I finished washing the tub and headed back to my room, the door opened, and it began. As the shoe plunged into my body, I was used to the pain already that tears no longer came so that night I forced them out, hoping she would see that she made my tears fall and she would stop. Eventually the beating stopped that night.

In those moments I found refuge in the red Bible which lay beside me on my bed. I would sleep with it every night on my chest. I was okay with the beatings as they represented the pins being buried into my skin. But the poisonous fumes became unfathomably overbearing. They not only entered my mind but triggered the snake to come into the box. The words she kept casting at me that I was useless, I had no mother, my father did not want me, I am a vagabond, I only like man business and fucking. These poisons became even more real to me when I looked around me and no one was there, and my father whom I had not seen yet, did not want me to live with him. Since my biological mother was in Africa, I was unable to speak with her every month.

The poison grew large one day, when my cousin, who in America was known as my brother, moved back in the house for a little bit. His girlfriend would come to visit him at times. One day I was in my room, and I heard my name being called by "Aunty Musu."

"Yes Mommy," I answered.

"Come here!" she insisted.

As I approached her, I knew I was in for it again. I didn't know for what really because I'd been in my room for most of the day. She told me to enter my brother's room, I did just that. Suddenly she raised a towel that had blood on it.

"So you're sleeping with him now; He finish virginizing you, you like man too much." I couldn't comprehend what she was saying or accusing me of or who she was talking about.

"I knew this was going to happen, you too fresh, now y'all na dirty my guest towel (Liberian English)?" I replied, with tears rolling down my cheeks, "Mommy I didn't do anything. Ronny didn't touch me I swear to God, I was in my room all day."

"I will take you to go get check, when they say anything that you been virginized I'm shipping your ass right back to Africa," she said.

It just so happened that my brother had walked through the door right at that moment, and when she asked him, he said, "Ay Mommy, why will you think like that? My own little sister? I didn't see Gloria all day; I'm just getting home. That's my girlfriend who came on her period, that's the blood you see on the towel."

Even though my brother said that the blood wasn't mine and his girlfriend later on came to affirm it, I knew I wasn't going free that easily. The beating came later on that night for something as tiny as cooking and not saying thank you. I was told to stop eating and throw the food away.

That week my brother decided he couldn't take much of what was going on in the house anymore and decided to move out. The moment he moved out that hole of escape for me became even more distant. It got much worse. I was no longer allowed to refer to my biological mother as "Mommy," nor was I to speak to my aunt Olu in public. I was not allowed to visit my neighbor who became my friend at school. If my friend ever made the mistake of knocking on our door to ask me to play, I would suffer the consequences. The black snake entered the box and I grew lonely, depressed, fragile and I felt like dying. My dreams would be more of nightmares. I would wake up from my sleep and believe that something or someone was lying next to me that I could not see. I began hearing voices to hurt myself. As much as I would hold my Bible to my chest, it was not enough because my mind was occupied with the voice of the snake, which made me feel as though I had someone to talk to. I began speaking back to the voice and at times we would talk for hours. I started being afraid of the dark because of the nightmares and not wanting to wake up to the thought of something in my room that I could not see with the lights off. By then my friend in my head was sharpening its teeth and I did not know that this bite was going to hurt me.

One morning, I was hurrying to get ready to go to school without waking up Aunt Musu. I was almost finished and ready to leave when Aunt Musu called me from the bathroom and asked me about the tub and why I took a bath and did not wash it. Knowing within myself that I did not take a shower that morning, there was no way that I could've been the one to dirty the tub. But I didn't want her to know that I didn't take a shower, so I lied and said I cleaned the tub. She pulled my ear in the bathroom and took me towards the tub.

"Mommy I didn't dirty the tub, I cleaned it."

Well that's exactly what I did that morning before school - I had to clean the tub. As I began heading towards the stairs, she called me back with a shoe in her hands and said it wasn't cleaned. I pleaded with her.

"Mommy please, I'm going to be late for school. I will clean it after school, please Mommy!"

She felt as though I was talking back to her and began to beat me with the shoe. With a sudden push down the stairs I fell and hit the little glass table at the bottom of the stairs. I ran towards the door.

"Come here! If you get me in trouble at that school ehn you will come meet me home." So I went off to school. After lunch time I was called to my guidance counselor's office. She would check on me daily. She noticed that I had a bruised knot on my head, so she asked me if everything was okay and how I got the knot. I told her I hit the door by accident. She asked if my mom knew this, and I said no. She decided to call home after I told her no one was home and that my mom was at work. She said she was going to leave a message. Turned out that Aunty Musu was still home, and after the guidance counselor spoke to her, she handed me the phone. She sounded angry and asked me if I was trying to get her in trouble. I said, "No Mommy."

She replied, "Just come meet me at home, you will see."

Those words sank in my chest. After school I was on my way home and suddenly I found myself scared and fearful of the beating I was in for. This was the first time I began the road to the 10%, the 18% and the 45%. The first moment of the sixty times that I would run away. I had nowhere to go and as I walked the streets, I ended up at my neighbor's house. Later, my neighbor told me to go home because it was getting too late. I went home and my present was waiting for me. I grew tired of it and my friend in my head was about to betray me, telling me to do something that I couldn't shake off not doing. It all made sense, so that very night after Aunty Musu went to bed, I snuck downstairs into the kitchen, opened the drawer of utensils, grabbed a knife with a brown handle and began to look at my wrist. It took me awhile to do it because I knew it might hurt, but the pain I was feeling from the poisonous fumes deteriorating my organs, the pins that stuck my body constantly was far worse than this, so I pierced the knife with a little quick gouge on my wrist as I wept. That night the vacuum of dust which entered the box consumed me.

I ran away constantly from home after that, although I knew the result that would await me at home in my box. I grew rebellious at school, filled with anger, and I almost entered a gang of girls. I was fighting in bathrooms, disrespecting teachers, and was kicked out of class. I began going out with a guy that wasn't good for me, and although I kept my grades up and was an honor roll student, I was going down a path that I felt like I couldn't control. The vacuum was sucking up all of my energy, my zeal, my strength, my positivity, and my beliefs. Everything that could save me was being sucked up by this vacuum, as the dirt consumed me, filling every airway up within. My self-esteem was lower than it should have been, and I felt dirty as the roaches crawled in and manipulated my beauty. I was only awaiting my saving grace, and soon I received a replica of it.

Chapter 7 - Slippery Slope of Trust

Things continued to go bad, and I started going from home to home because Aunty Musu began working different shifts that made her not be home as much, or when she got home I would be at school. For me it was a relief to be at her friend's place and feeling some kind of freedom. I was still a good kid and respectful to my African elders, although within I was angry and depressed. I would spend nights and weekends at Aunty Musu's friend's house, but I loved it when I was allowed to spend the night at Aunty Musu's son's home. Her son and his wife noticed that I was very happy being there with them, and I honestly was happy. I felt loved and trusted, and everything good. There was discipline, we did chores, and we prayed and went to church; it was a family. I was gradually losing my snakes and I felt that gradually I had been removed from the box. I couldn't do it myself and they were helping. My cousin and his wife asked Aunty Musu if I could stay with them, and Aunty Musu agreed. I still went to my same school by taking the public bus every morning between the ages ten to twelve. Sometimes I would get dropped off if I missed the bus. I didn't mind the distance and time it took to arrive at school because it felt good being loved, I thought. I had friends and was in a praise dance group. I stopped being so bad at school. And suddenly it all changed. This roller coaster was soon about to reach its peak and spiral downwards.

At about 1:00am one morning, there was a knock on the front door, one after the other. How come nobody heard it but me? The entire house was silent. "Knock, knock." There it went again.

I couldn't ignore it and if I tried to I couldn't sleep through it. So I got out of bed, left my cousin inside, and went to open the door. The living room was dim from the only light that shone from the top of the stairs. I was sleepy, with my eyes still halfway closed. I approached the door and saw uncle Morris, (my aunt Helen by marriage brother). I opened the door to let him in. I made sure the door was locked behind us. As I locked the front door, Uncle Morris was already sitting on the couch. I was so tired and didn't bother to pay attention to his demeanor, so I hurried back upstairs to bed. Almost at the very top of the stairs with only four more steps to go, I heard Uncle Morris's voice calling me. "Hey, come here."

"Yes Uncle Morris, you called me?" I was rubbing my sleepy eyes to indicate how sleepy I was.

He asked, "Everyone sleeping?"

I said "Yes. I was sleeping too but I heard the door."

"Okay," he said. I began heading back up the stairs.

"Goodnight," I said to him.

As I turned around he said, "Come here, go get me the Vaseline."

Not knowing his reasons for the Vaseline, I followed his directions and went into the dining room to get the Vaseline. I managed to locate the Vaseline under the wooden baby bed. Suddenly as I went back into the living room to hand Uncle Morris the Vaseline, my eyes were in awe and my heartbeats simultaneously grew faster. I stood still, not knowing what to do. There stood before me Uncle Morris's penis from his trousers.

As he stroked it, the only words I could utter was, "I have to go to bed." He grabbed my arm with the Vaseline and told me to rub

Then aunt Helen said, "Okay, as long as you are sure, we will ask Morris what happened that night."

I was in shock; I didn't know what to say. My twelve-year-old mind shut down. I was in complete shock. I simply replied, "Okay" and went upstairs as fast as I could in disbelief, not processing what the disbelief was about in my mind or what the shock pertained to.

The next day, at around 4pm, I was called to the same spot as the previous day. There sat Aunty Helen and Uncle Lee. Aunt Helen prompted me to sit in a chair in the middle as uncle Lee was looking in his book.

She said: "We heard what you said yesterday and asked Morris. He said that he never open his trousers or took out anything. He said he would never do that. Even though he was drunk when he came home, nothing happened like that. But we want to say if it did happen we're sorry."

At that very moment on hearing those words, I felt numb. That must have been my very first heartbreak since leaving Liberia.

"So you don't believe me?" I asked both aunt Helen and Uncle Lee. "Are you backing him because he's your brother?"

"She replied; no Gloria; it's just hard because he denied it happening and said he doesn't remember, that he will not do something like that, so what do you want us to do?"

I couldn't cry anymore. I think I had run out of tears, and it became anger. Still being obedient as a child, I let that night go as the memories lingered in my mind, eating at my flesh. One thing I was left with from that encounter was the beginning of a trustless life. I became one that would never again trust those closest to me. The ones who loved me, the ones with whom I felt the happiest with, the ones who made me feel like I was a child in a family, the ones whom I looked up to for peace, love and serenity, broke my heart.

Although I was heartbroken and unable to trust those close to me again, I stayed with Uncle Lee and Aunt Helen. I was still actively involved in the dance group that Aunt Helen created with my friends. Everything was similar to what it used to be. My behavior changed a little towards Uncle Lee, especially when he tried to discipline me. Without knowing why, I felt he had no right to do it anymore. Not knowing how long I would be with Aunt Helen and Uncle Lee, I forgot about going back to live with Aunt Musu until she surprised us one afternoon. Aunt Musu came to take me back, and I dared not question why. I later found out it was because she and Uncle Lee and Aunt Helen were not on good terms for something having to do with car insurance. I left Aunt Helen and Uncle Lee's house that day at age thirteen. It wasn't until later in my life when I realized how much my trust in others was damaged.

Chapter 8 - Final Run

We arrived at aunt Musu's house, which I probably should call home. Nothing had changed; everything was still the same. I felt like I never left, and gradually I began to remember my daily routines. What did change was that I would spend more time in my room than ever before, trying to avoid any confrontation. I felt a little lighter, and less afraid. Something felt different this time being in the home. I couldn't gather what it was, but I would soon find out.

Although there was something different about being at home this time around, one thing that did not change was the beatings and words towards me. I remember calling Uncle Lee and telling him how tired I was with how I was being treated. I finally felt as though I had a voice and some kind of strength in me. This time was definitely different. I was unsure if it was because I didn't care about much anymore in my life or if because I received a taste of what affection and love was and lost it. Whatever it was, there was nothing else to lose.

It was a Saturday morning and Aunty Musu was home. I could overhear her in her room quarreling about something. Then, "Gloria!" she called out. Was she really calling me?

"Gloria!"

"Yes Mommy," I replied, while going into her room. "Mommy you called me?"

"Who went through my jewelry and use my good good perfumes?"

"I don't know Mommy, It wasn't me."

I remember the day before she sent me to go and get her fabric from her room, but I touched nothing else.

"So I was the one who came and scatter my own things ehn," she questioned me.

I kept silent.

"Get from my face and go clean the place."

Leaving her room with relief, I began to gather the cleaning supplies to clean the house. I cleaned upstairs first, then I vacuumed and went downstairs. After wiping down everything downstairs, I washed the dishes. As I turned on the vacuum downstairs, Aunt Musu called me back upstairs into the bathroom.

"Did you clean this bathroom?"

"Yes Mommy."

"Come here," she pushed my head down into the tub and then pulled my ear towards the sink, "You didn't clean this bathroom."

"Mommy I did."

"Shut up your mouth. Go get the cleaning things and come clean this bathroom so I can take a bath. I went back downstairs to get the cleaning supplies. A sudden thought came to my head and wouldn't go away. I made the decision that would change my life forever. It only took that one decision to meet my saving grace - the real saving grace.

****
****
****

As Aunt Musu went back into her room as she waited for the bathroom, I tiptoed back up the stairs. Halfway up the stairs it began to squeak.

"Oh no, I can't let her see me." So, I went back down the first half of the stairs slowly. I had to think of another way. It was cold outside, and I could hear her walking around upstairs. So I went into the basement door and grabbed the first coat I could see with my slippers already on my feet. I quickly wrote a note of "I'm sorry Mommy" and did what I knew best. Slowly I opened the front door, trying to prevent it from squeaking. A few minutes later I was out the door. I had ran away, but this time was different. This time would be the last, but the first into my new journey. I was about to experience a chapter of my life that I never thought was possible.

I walked and walked and didn't know where I was going. I found myself going towards the direction of Aunt Musu ex-husband house, my family who were living in the home together with Aunt Musu and I before leaving. I missed them and thought that would be the last place that aunt Musu would look for me. As I arrived standing at the door for some minutes contemplating if I should disturb them with my problems, wondering what if they called "Mommy" and tell her where I am? We were all afraid so they might be scared to even have me over. I let all the thoughts out of my head and knocked twice, and then another two knocks. The door opened. It was my female cousin, one of the younger ones who were the last to leave with her dad, who we all call "Pa." To this day I still call him "Pa."

But Pa wasn't home at the time and I was extremely glad for that, because he definitely would have called Aunt Musu right away. So I stepped in the home with the big black coat on me.

"Gloria what you doing here (Liberian English)?" She asked. "Does Mommy know you're here?"

"I can't go back there; I'm not going back," I replied.

Then my other cousin who's a bit older and was amongst the first group of guys to leave involuntarily came downstairs to hear what was going on.

"Oh Gloria you're here, why you got that big coat on? (laughing)."

"It's "Mommy" coat, I couldn't grab my own so I took hers," I said.

They started laughing and I smiled.

"So are you going back or staying here?" he asked

"I'm not going back."

"You know she's going to find out you're here and come for you, right?" I had hoped he wouldn't remind me of that, but he was probably right. Of course she was going to find me there, but for that moment I felt safe, and it would take hours before she would figure out where I was. I told my cousins that I wasn't going back and they shouldn't allow me to go back.

"Gloria we know how mommy is, but you know you just have to hold your heart and bear it small until you reach eighteen and can leave," he said.

"I can't bear it for that long. Y'all don't understand what has been going on at least here y'all altogether and Pa is not like Mommy. There's some kind of freedom. Y'all were able to leave with Pa, but me I couldn't. I'm not going back; I'm tired (tears running down my cheeks)."

My other little male cousin came down the stairs, surprised as the other two were. "(Liberian English) Oh what you doing here? (smiling) Mommy know you here?" the constant surprise and repeated questions had me smiling.

"You better go home before le catch you here and beat you."

Me: "When mommy come to that door I'm not here ooh." (We all laughed.)

"You know Mommy, I scared of her," he said.

Then my big cousin said, "You can stay here until Pa comes and we tell him what's going on."

I stayed and went in the kitchen to my girl cousin who was cooking cabbage at the time. That was when I first learned to cook my first soup. After the cabbage was done and I was about to fix something to eat, there was a knock at the door. My heart started suddenly beating faster as the minutes and knock kept coming. My little male cousin came downstairs asking, "Who's that?" as my older cousin went to the window to check. "It's Mommy," he said.

My little cousin ran upstairs as quick as possible saying, "I told y'all I'm not here."

My other female cousin said, "Aahh she's here ooh, maybe she will go if no one answers." My older cousin still thinking what to do. "But she saw me opening the window curtain, she know we here."

"Then open the door now," she said back to him.

"Please don't open it," I asked him.

"Y'all open this door before I call the police," we all heard "Mommy" say from the opposite side of the door.

So he ended up opening the door and you could see everyone's heart pounding from under their clothing as we all said, "Hi Mommy."

"(Liberian English), What you doing here, ehn? What are you doing here, come on get your ass out, let's go!" Aunt Musu said as she pointed towards the door. I stood there quiet and didn't utter a word nor did I move an inch.

"I'm talking to you, if you don't leave this house I will call the police and they will lock you up and I will send your ass back to Africa," she explained.

As she continued speaking, "I know you came here for man business, (pointing to my older guy cousin), but if you want man go find man somewhere else, now get out."

"I'm not going back with you." As I uttered the words out of my mouth, I could see the shock on everyone's face. We were all waiting for the heavy smack across my face. But it didn't happen.

"If I leave this place, and you're not in that car with me, just know all of y'all getting in trouble with the police. Her ass going to juvenile prison and then ship back to Africa and for letting her inside this place that's a charge for y'all."

We knew nothing about the law and I'm pretty sure that was all incorrect information she was giving us, but as naive as we were, we somehow believed it. Aunt Musu left the house and went outside into her car. My cousins persuaded me to go with her and I went to meet her in the car. It was a short ten-minute ride filled with silence and anger that made it seemed longer than it was. As we arrived home I went directly upstairs to my room. Ten minutes later I heard Aunt Musu on the phone, so I came out and sat at the top of the stairs. She was on the phone with my father who lived out of state. After a long conversation with him, she called me downstairs and handed me the phone.

Me: "Hi Daddy."

Him: "Hi Gloria, how you doing?"

Me: "Not good."

Him: "I know, so your aunty and I just spoke and she told me what's been going on, and that you want to put her in trouble. She said you don't want to live with her anymore; is that true?"

Me: "Yes."

Him: "Okay so, what I want you do for me is to write a letter, telling her thank you and how you appreciate her, but in that letter let her know where you think will be best for you to go live. Let her know where you want to go live, okay honey? Because is either that or she sends you back to Africa to your mom. Do you want to go back to Africa?"

Me: "No (I honestly wanted to say yes). "No," was on my tongue automatically, with no explanation behind it.

Him: "Okay, then please write the letter so we can know where you feel will be best for you to be until you turn eighteen. Because Your aunty say you don't want to be with her anymore and I myself can't take you. Now she don't want you there either before you put her in trouble."

Me: "Okay, but I don't want to put her in trouble."

Him: "Okay Ma, I understand . Please write the letter okay, then we will take it from there. And tell her sorry."

Me: "Okay Daddy."

Him: "Thank you, ma."

I gave the phone back to Aunt Musu and went upstairs to write the letter. I wrote a three page double-sided letter on yellow paper, expressing myself and following the directing of my father. In the letter I thanked Aunt Musu and apologized to her, not because my father told me to; I sincerely meant every word that I wrote. When I wrote the list of people who I felt would take me in, mainly only three places I could think of, and the first place that was emphasized in the letter was her son's place, where I stayed and felt the most wanted and loved, the place where she had no idea about what had happened with Uncle Morris and me. Despite what happened, I still wanted to go and live there because it's where I honestly at the time felt the most happiest, the most family togetherness and I had friends. I wanted that feeling back; I yearned for that peace again, and writing their names in this letter was my opportunity to regain a family. I also put my aunt Mandy on the list where my grandmother was staying as well. I felt that my grandmother loved me so much that staying where she was would be wonderful and I would be happy. I explained my reasons for choosing those two places and with confidence I knew I would be wanted by the people I listed. But I also put on the list a third option for a just in case, and that was my aunt Olu. Her name was barely on the paper; there was no explanation behind why I chose her name because I did not think there was a possibility of me residing with her, nor did I even believe I would be allowed to. I wrote her name, just in case.

Before the day ended I handed Aunt Musu the letter when she came home. I told her that I was sorry for everything, and she took the letter from my hand. She read it later and the next day after her morning shift at work she called me downstairs.

She said she had read what I wrote. Then she told me unfortunately I could not go to live with her son. She mentioned that she would not allow it, and because that is her son so if I'm not living with her then I cannot live with her son, so I should root it out of my head. Then she explained to me how my aunt Mandy do not want me to live with her because I was a troublemaker and she heard of all the things I did at school and she didn't want me to put her in trouble. I was devastated and heartbroken with nowhere to go, and my father was out of the question. He had already told me I couldn't live with him. I had forgotten about my third option "Aunt Olu." Aunt Musu continued speaking as I dozed off in disappointment.

"So I am going to call your Dad and let him know that I'm sending you back to Africa."

Aunt Musu called my father that day and they talked for almost an hour. The next day she called me downstairs and handed me the phone. It was my father on the phone. He asked me about the letter and what was said in it, and also talked about the names I wrote about where I want to stay. He told me that Aunty Musu's decision to not allow me to stay with her son and his wife, and Aunty Mandy's decision to not let me stay with her was final. So the only option was to send me to Africa, but he called Aunty Olu to tell her that I was going to be sent back to Africa and she suggested to him that she will take me into her home. He asked me if I want to go to Africa or to Aunty Olu. Then I remembered putting her as my last option and it turned out she wanted to take me into her home. I know that I had been to her house once with grandma when I went to visit grandma after school one day. I knew I would see my grandma everyday now. I do not know what or how it happened, but I am grateful it did.

I ended up going to Aunty Olu's house (age 13 1/2). She lived in a two bedroom apartment with her three kids and her daughter's father, with grandma visiting every day. This journey had just gotten interesting. The next phase I was about to enter was not expected ... but it had to happen for me to reach where I am presently.

Chapter 9 - Angry Bird Extension

School became a safe haven. No matter what was going on around me, school was the only consistent thing I looked forward to every day. It was an escape. No matter what awaited for me at school, I preferred to face them than stay home. There was another survival obstacle at school. From 6th to 7th grade, the friends I had were far from the kinds of children that an average parent would want their child to have as friends. I cared, yet I didn't. I was growing into someone who was unrecognizable. There was no hope anymore. There was still that voice in my head wanting to stop the chaos I was slowly getting myself into, but its counterpart became stronger. Filled with frustration, anger, hopelessness and rage the four overpowered the one voice that stood alone. The majority won.

I became rebellious in classes, and I was getting kicked out of class just like most of the others. I began imitating the leader of the new girl gang. She told us to call her "Princess." We all knew her real name, well at least I did, but I called her what she wished because I was afraid of getting beat up. There was a routine where in order to join you will have to hang out with the group, and the initiation began after fighting another female in the girls' bathroom. I witnessed a few of the initiation fights in the girls' bathroom. One of their noses bleed so much and I felt powerless, afraid that if I left or reported it, I too would look as she did. After the fight the two girls would clean themselves up and stay in the bathroom until they felt "normal" again to come out. Sometimes it took hours. Teachers would ask and no one will say where the girls were. They would eventually come out the bathroom and join the rest of us. It was about three weeks into me hanging out with the group. I was kicked out of classes. I talked back to teachers, and I was banging on classroom windows with a ring I wore. It was my turn to fight. "Princess" found a another female who I'd never seen before in the group of girls, and that's when I began second-guessing if being "bad" or a part of this group was really what I wanted. We all stepped in the bathroom, nervous and sweaty hands. "Was I really about to fight? If I don't they'll just beat me up," I was thinking to myself.

"Okay, you two fight," Princess said.

I stood there while the other girl got ready to hit me. "Come on 'bitch,' let's go ... or you scared or something?" She asked me.

"I'm not scared."

"Well then, let's go." She hit me and I hit her back saying, "Stop ... I don't want to fight." "Then you can't hang with us, and you don't have friends anyway so you going to be all alone," Princess said.

"Well I don't want to fight or be a part of your stupid gang." I don't know what in the world was coming out of my mouth, but the words kept coming, scared as I was.

"If y'all touch me I'll tell, and all y'all gonna get in trouble."

"Ain't nobody care about getting in trouble; you funny as hell, but you know what, I didn't like you anyway so you not even worth being in my gang; but watch your back African booty scratcher," Princess said while in my face.

With relief they left me in the bathroom. I stayed there for what seemed like forever, but it was about thirty minutes. When I went back to class, it was already over. We had to switch to our next class. Princess passed next to me and tripped me.

"You know what Amarie, I'm sick and tired of you. You real name not even Princess. Who made you Princess? Your name is Amarie and that's exactly what I'm going to call you A.m.a.r.i.e."

She got in my face. "You better not call me that."

"Watch me. I'm African, remember, so don't even try to fight me."

After that, I knew that Amarie (Princess) was actually scared of me and although I was scared of getting jumped by her and her gang, I didn't care at the moment. The rest of the school year was spent with me avoiding Amarie and her crew and fighting other girls and boys who picked on me, insulted my mother and called me African booty scratcher constantly. I ended up getting into seven fights in total in my middle school years (three boys, four girls). Before I was transferred to a new school in the area where my aunt Olu lived, the last weeks at that school were unreal. My 6th grade social studies teacher saw me eating a chocolate bar.

"Gloria put the candy away."

"No Miss. A I need it."

"GLORIA PUT IT AWAY NOW."

"Why are you yelling? It's just candy, it's not bothering you."

"You either put it away or give it to me."

"Okay fine, I'm not going to eat it, but I need it."

"For what? She asked.

"I have low blood and low sugar - unless you want me to die."

"Gloria put it away you will be just fine."

"Can I use the bathroom?" I asked her.

I left to use the bathroom. When I came back, my fifty-cent candy was gone. "Where's my candy? Who took my candy?"

"Ooo Ms. A took your candy," someone said. After finding out Ms. A took my candy, I went to Ms. A asking her for my candy, and she refused to give it to me and insisted that I sit down. Of course I refused. I walked behind Ms. A everywhere she went in the classroom asking her for my candy. She wouldn't give it to me, so I began throwing books and the Legos she had out for us that day. She threatened to call the security guard to take me to in-school suspension. I told her I didn't care as long as she gave me my candy. She grabbed the phone to call the main office for the security guards while I still insisted on getting my candy. I was getting closer to her (Ms. A and I was about the same height). She must've been surprised and scared that day. I was an honor roll student and didn't really talk in her class before. I could see the shock and fear on her face, but yet I couldn't make myself stop. I reached for her hand to grab the candy from it.

"Gloria sit down!" she yelled.

I repeated what she said, adding: "Just give me my candy. You started this by taking my candy. I was not bothering you and now I want it back."

It took ten minutes before the security came with the principal and took me to the In-School Suspension (ISS) room. I told the principal what happened. They called my aunt Olu and I went to ISS. On the phone with Aunt Olu I told her to allow my dad and aunt Musu to send me back to Africa. She laughed and I wasn't sure why. I was to get suspended for seven days but because my cousins and I went to the same school and we had never been suspended before, my cousin's dad came to talk to the principal, I stayed in ISS for two days instead.

Chapter 10 - The "S" Attempts

Suicide is real. It's been a topic that a lot of us are ashamed to talk about and ashamed to acknowledge. It's almost as though we don't want to believe that someone is capable of taking their own life and they may seem perfectly fine before they do it. Suicide is something that we all need to talk about, because talking about it might save a life. Talking about suicide might bring forth provisions to prevent it, to help those who may be on the verge of committing suicide. Even within religion, suicide exists, whether if it's done as a sacrifice to save lives or to aquit for a mistake or betrayal (Judas in the Bible). I believe the important question that we are unable to wrap our heads around in understanding is "Why?" and being afraid of accepting the answers to why someone will take their own life usually makes us not want to talk about it. But acknowledging its existence will only help to remove its stigma and the existing problem in many areas.

Usually suicide doesn't just happen; it forms over a period of time. It begins as a seed planted and then it is watered by things, by the people, by ideas, by perceptions, thoughts and feelings, and by personal emotions. All of these are what water the thought of suicide. And just as a plant grows when it is watered, it also needs some light to sprout to become healthy. So, for the individual, the light they see or need shines through, but it becomes distorted and confused with the form of the lights from the other side, instead of the sunlight from life here on earth. That's when suicide happens.

During my journey of becoming who I am today, and during this process of life, taking my own life was an option. My only light to freeing myself became distorted. In fact I felt it was always an option. That's the thing where being negative is always an option and being positive is always an option. Living is always an option, just as dying by your own hands presents itself as an option, and most people are unaware of this. I sought out the option of dying several times, specifically six times it creeped up on me. It began as a tiny planted seed. Although I may try to describe the feeling of how it crept up on me, my description is not close to the weight I felt during each time that I tried to take my own life. The smile that has been described in the last five years of my life that people see was not always there. The smile that is shown now is real. Yet, in the past, my heart was filled with misbelief that reflected a damaged soul, damaged heart, damaged mind, and a damaged spirit. I remember the loneliness as it crept up every now and then. I'm African, so we don't believe in depression, bipolar disorder nor delusions unless it's a spirit for religious purposes. There is a lot of mental health issues that we don't believe in. So for me to say that I had depression or that I had perhaps a mental illness that would be inaccurate. What is accurate is that one minute I was happy, then the next I was extremely angry and then excited, then confused and happy. Feelings of anxiety and anxious thoughts would run through my head as the tears fell. I fought hard [not] to escape from my own thoughts. What I can say or describe is the motion, the feelings, and the turmoil. I felt as though I was sinking in the quicksand, with my chest tightening, my stomach tightening, my heart pounding one moment and suddenly slowing down, gasping for air but couldn't find it because it was infected with turmoil. The quicksand sucked down my body, and then I couldn't fight it anymore. I decided to just let go. I couldn't scream anymore, and I couldn't cry anymore. Although the tears still came, they came without permission. I felt lost and hopeless. I had no reason to live, no one to talk to, no one to trust. I thought that I was going to be a burden. I was rejected by those around me, and I felt like I was a disappointment every time I was by myself. Those around me couldn't help me. The physical, mental, and emotional abuse did not help the situation either. Where was this God that I once believed in? In my teenage mind, He did not care. If He did, He would not have allowed the things to happen that happened. There were no other visible options that were running across my mind but that one option of taking myself out of the equation of life. There were other options that now I realize were there at the time, but they were buried beneath the negative thoughts. It was hidden by darkness and I had to find something in order to reach the sunlight. The sunlight came later, but at that moment it wasn't bright enough.

It was 2011, and the temperature was about fifty degrees, not too warm but mildly chilly at about 11:00pm.

"Gloria I am going to leave you here with the little boy. His mom coming to pick him up. Watch him because he likes to leave the house."

"Dale , don't leave le people son with me please, I have problems of my own and I can't watch anyone child in the state I'm in."

"It's just for thirty minutes; you will be okay. Jes keep him upstairs. He's sleeping right now seh."

Dale left the house with that last response. In my mind I was already panicking. I was not in the mood to watch anyone's kid. I went upstairs after twenty minutes of Dale's leaving me in the living room. The boy was lying there so lifelessly. He looked as though he was in another realm. He had no sense of what was going on in my reality. He looked about six to seven years old. Neither he or I would fathom what was to come next. As he peacefully slept I went back downstairs. Suddenly an outburst of fear and sadness overtook me as a match suddenly exploding with blazing beams. I needed a walk. I needed fresh air; I needed to breathe. Thoughts were flying everywhere. I told my brother I was not up to this; I told him not to leave me with this child. I told him but he couldn't listen. He didn't hear what I was saying. I can't do this.

"I don't belong here. Why am I here? Lord, why?"

The door was now open, as I sat halfway in and halfway out the house. I was trying to calm my racing thoughts down. Five minutes went by. Ten minutes later, the door closed with me on the outside of it. Slowly making a right, I walked and walked.

"I just want it all to be over; I'm tired," I said to myself as the tears flowed. I knew what was happening (or did I really?). I was feeling numb without a care in the world of what would happen next. I slowly approached the street. Where was I going? My mind could not tell me to stop as my feet moved along with the adrenaline. I was emotionless. I couldn't even feel my body that was about to be taken away. I felt like I had no spirit, no soul; it was as though I was being carried. It was all about to be over, releasing everyone of it; no more burdens from me. I mean, no one cared anyway, and for those who said they did I did not trust that it was genuine. There was no strength in me to even try to believe that they did. Nothing was being left behind because there was nothing: any hope, joy, happiness, peace or love. Nothing at that moment in my mind as I was approaching … almost there … the road. It's so close, it's your freedom, your peace.

"Just sit there, don't move," the voice said. "Just do it."

That's what I did, hoping that this would be the end and that moment would be the last. No one would have to worry about taking care of me. No one will have to think about sending me to school nor would they have to fight for me to keep me stable. Family members would not have to argue about me again. Everyone would be happy and all the pain and hurt that I caused them would be forgotten. And wherever I will be going to will probably be a lot better than where I was. I sat there in the middle of the road and waited with my eyes closed. Nothing came, so I stood up the cement road beneath me, as my feet clenched tight, I waited for cars or something to come.

"God please help me, I need your help, take me now to You. I don't want to hurt them. I don't want to be a burden to her; please God."

No cars, nothing. I stood there for probably a good thirty minutes, and then I decided to sit, and still nothing. Nothing, absolutely nothing; nothing came. Nothing at all. No cars, no trucks, no moving object came to take me away. The thirty minutes felt like forever. I was in the middle of that street just waiting for some car to come and bang me, piercing my tiny bones. It was absolutely silent ... So I sat down and closed my eyes again. I was disappointed when I heard the voices call out my name this time. It was real voices from my aunt and my brother looking for me. As I came back to reality, reality still had me numb. Somehow the strength came. I slowly turned away from the road like nothing happened. If only a car would've came that night and made something happen, I probably wouldn't have had to lie to Aunty Olu about where I came from. Suddenly I heard Dale call my name.

"Gloria, Gloria" Gloria, where are you???"

With no rush or quickness in my movements, I slowly wiped my face with my hands and got up, little to no zeal to comprehend why Dale was yelling my name as late as it was. As I approached the house, Dale saw me coming towards him.

"Gloria, where is the le boy?"

"I left him inside sleeping upstairs," I told him.

Dale: "Well he's not there. I came and met the door open. I told you to watch him because he luh leave the house without people knowing."

At this time I noticed my cousin Munde with Dale. I guess he came back with Dale from wherever they came from at this time of the night.

"Honestly Dale, I told you not to leave him with me, why would you even leave a child with me after you know I'm not in the right frame of mind with everything that's been going on? You know why I came here, and that was not to watch anybody child, especially someone that can just leave the house like that. Where does he usually go when he leaves the house?" I asked.

Dale said he didn't know, that's just what the child's mother told him." We looked for the boy for what seemed to be twenty minutes, tops. I decided to go and take a breather and set out to the backroom where no one could know, and there was the little boy in the back watching TV.

"He's in the back here!" I yelled to them.

Munde called the boy. "Where you coming from, you didn't hear us calling your name, looking for you all over this place here?" The child shook his head "no."

"Don't do it next time you hear me?" said Munde. He received another head nod, but this time he indicated "yes."

Munde sent the child back to sleep, which was probably about 3am. I remained in the back room, and then I heard my name once again. I came to see who was calling me. I entered the living room and saw Munde and Dale sitting down. I already knew what was about to be said. I didn't bother to sit. I stood on the side, waiting for their questions of where I went and why.

Munde: "Where did you go, and why did you leave after knowing that they le boy was here and that he could run leave. Didn't Dale tell you? Don't you think that was very selfish? I'm very disappointed in you Gloria."

What was I to say now, I thought? Meanwhile, in another part of my mind I did not care at all; I was living aimlessly and couldn't give a damn about anyone's emotions or words at that very moment. I was tired of it all and wanted them to know my emotions and thoughts. Wanting to feel something along the lines of remorse or care, searching to feel empathy and trying to accept the blame on myself was hidden in a nail stack of pain and dysfunction and all that I saw was the emotional dysfunction.

My response to Munde: "I don't know Munde, sorry. I went for a walk. I told Dale not to leave the boy with me because honestly I did not come here to babysit. I came here to get away from some of the chaos and noise at home. I think it was unfair for him to do that and now want to blame me for le boy leaving the house or disappearing? I don't even know le people son or his people. Y'all brave seh. To leave any child with someone like me right now. I'm going to go to sleep now. I'm tired of all this. I wish it was all over, seriously. We now find the boy so y'all please leave me."

I saw myself entering into what is culturally seen as disrespectful talk and didn't know how to slow it all down. When your mind is uncontrollable it's hard to tell what is happening to the brain, but what was happening to my brain was not my concern at that moment.

Munde didn't have much else to say after my response and he let me go. But that was not the last time. I tried again and again and again. I lived with the thoughts on and off, and I couldn't speak out; I couldn't confess it. As I said, African people won't believe you. They will say that you are just looking for attention, you're faking. I can tell you now that depression is real, and mental health Is real.

I remember one of those occasions, one of the attempts when my aunt finally got a clue and decided to take me for help, but while we were on the way in the car, all I could think about was another car coming into us. But not ending their lives, just ending mine. I imagined it happening. I had hoped it happened, but it didn't. I was so disappointed. The result of that night was I returned home, with no help.

[My most recent episode, written in my journal (2017).]

"I feel as though I'm going through this alone. I'm going through this and honestly it's nobody's fault I feel weak. This might be a weakness that I shouldn't be feeling this way. I should probably just hold on to God. I pray and that hasn't been helping. The feeling comes and goes away. I thought I was done with this feeling; why does it keep coming back and I should be happy? I know I should be. I'm in grad school, and a lot of people don't get to this level of a job, of an apartment of my own, both my parents are alive, I have friends and I have a boyfriend, so why do I feel so lonely? Why do I feel like I'm not doing anything right, and why do I feel like I haven't accomplished anything? Why do I feel like not being a part of this anymore? I know I'm not gonna do it. If I was, I would've done it by now. As I'm sitting here that was in my head to do it. There's three bottles of medicine on my table and a freaking bottled water sitting at the window. How did this combination in this moment seem to just appear right in front of me? My thoughts are going wild. I can't stop looking at the images in my head of how it will feel like to just take those medications with that stupid water. Why is this happening to me? Am I being selfish? And the plan that God has for me, I try; I try. Just the irony of it all is I'm preparing a presentation right now on freaking suicide but I'm not ... I am not going to give in to it. These thoughts are not real. I am stronger. I am wiser, and I am blessed and God has a plan for my life. The devil will not win this battle. I don't care; I know the tears will come. I know those moments will come where I feel depressed when I feel lonely. I feel that I am not accomplished; what I feel is that I cannot. Thoughts will come, but I will not ... I will not give in to what Satan wants me to do. I am a winner and I'm a believer. I'm more powerful than what my mind tells me at this moment. I'm stronger than what my impulses wants me to do at this moment. I am blessed indeed; it's okay to feel down a bit down, but I must pick myself back up. I know this feeling will return soon but once again. I will pick myself up again. I am loved by my friends and my family and my peers, and I am loved by myself. I will not end my happiness on this earth. God is the only one that will make that decision to call me home to Him when He is ready for me. Get up, shake it out and smile." [2017- 6:20pm to 6:38pm]

Things started turning around before I went to college. This was not as much of a turnaround as it was a step forward. Saying that God has been holding on to me is an understatement. I'm so sure I let go a long time ago, and if He wasn't holding on I wouldn't be doing what I am doing at this moment. The healing process began when I turned nineteen. During my first year in college, I was invited to church by a friend Lamar. He didn't know how much I needed that invitation and how much it changed my life. I believe that God sent him, and even through everything that happened, somehow I still knew that there was a God and I wanted to understand Him more to find out why things happened in certain ways. I made it through those times of suicidal thoughts and my happiness deepened. I shared that happiness by giving that same smile and that's from an encouraging place. Putting a smile on a stranger's face became a normal process for me to love and not give up. Do I still have days where I cry? Yes, I still have days where I feel lonely. Yes, I still have days where my thoughts wander on leaving this earth, but I'm in control now. God is in control now. One thing that I love right now is my life. I truly believe that I was born for a reason, and for that purpose of being born I have to be alive to achieve it. Nothing, nothing will influence me to ever want to take my life again.

For others who are not privileged to have the relationship that I had and still have with God, once again, one thousand options were there, yet He's always there for those who need and want Him. And for the individuals who were successful in taking their own lives, may their souls rest in perfect peace. Sorry to the families. For everyone else who has reached this point in this book, even if you don't believe in God, morals exist, and one of the main godly things on this Earth is kindness. It is morally right to show kindness as it may be someone's last lifeline to his/her smile. I'm praying that the cycle of suicide is turned.

happen when you have sex before age sixteen. Plus I was scared, honestly. I believe I still had some common sense in me. So I told him that we should wait. He asked until when and I would say, just waits. I mean he was a virgin too so he didn't push or force anything. So we waited until I turned sixteen, and nothing happened because I was still scared. I wasn't sure why I was about to have sex with him. To be honest, I couldn't remember anyone really trying to stop me or to tell me not to do it, and I was afraid to even bring up the topic at home. My aunt was free in talking about the topic, yet I did not want to be judged and my trust issues were high. I knew people were having sex at school; at least some of my friends were. But that wasn't why I wanted to. It was more to please him so he couldn't break up with me and leave me alone. But because I was so scared and afraid of what would happen, I asked him to wait because I wasn't ready. So we waited until we were together for nine months. Every time I went over to his house to hang out, he was with his friends. I will see them staring at me or maybe I was paranoid. I mean I started to love him and felt that he loved me; at least that's what he told me.

It was a normal day, just like any other walking the dog day, just going over his house. His siblings were home. We went upstairs, and I wasn't sure if I was even ready for that. We sat there and talked, and the next thing I knew, talking turned into kissing and making out, and then he pulled out a condom and it happened. I couldn't stop crying and I didn't know why. He asked me if I was okay and I said yes, but I really was not. I lost my virginity and there was no turning back. I tried to convince myself that that was okay because he was a virgin too and I had waited until I was seventeen. Plus, he loved me and I loved him, so I convinced myself that what happened was okay. Well, that happened about four more times, and each time I cried. I still didn't know why. What I did know was that something wasn't right. Two months later we ended up breaking up over something stupid as him not wanting to take me to his prom. I ended up being asked to go by someone else, but surprisingly the guy I went with was not my second encounter. No, my second time was much more complicated.

Still seventeen years old, almost eighteen. My aunt had a friend who had three sons. So, her friend came to visit and brought two of the sons with her; the older one and the little one. I was in my room studying I believe, but as an African custom, out of respect I went to the living room to speak and say hi. I was not focused on either son. I spoke and went back to the room. Then about thirty minutes had passed and the older one came to ask for the bathroom. I showed him and went back to the room. On his way back from the bathroom he stood at the door of my room and was very pleasant. He asked me about school and I replied pleasantly as well. Then he asked me for my aunt's number saying that my aunt told him to ask me for her number to write it down for him. So as naïve as I could be, he asked him just in case I don't get in touch with your aunt can you please give me your number as well? I really thought that that was the reason why he was asking for my number, to get in touch with my aunt because she is well known to not pick up her phone. He took it and then not too long after that they left the house. I told my aunt I gave him the numbers. That's when she began to tell me that he's a nice person, very intelligent and so on and so forth. I mentioned to her that I wasn't interested and plus I didn't think he was cute. She would reply it's not about being cute; he loves school and is very smart and is respectful and that she sees all of her friends' sons as her sons. I didn't really pay mind to it until two days later I received a phone call. He said that he was just calling to check on me to see how I was doing. I told him that was very nice of him and that I was doing very well. Due to my disinterest in him, the conversation wasn't very long. Now I'm a sucker for niceness but I still wasn't interested in this guy. Gradually he would come over without his mom to visit my aunt; well so I thought. I learned later that the visits were actually meant to get my attention.

To fast-forward the story, I ended up giving him a chance but all he talked about was school which is nice, but I already knew that school was the only way for me. At this time, I was 17 1/2 and we had been hanging out with each other and talking for about two years. He was very respectful but somehow, I just wasn't interested. Nothing sexual happened between us. By this time my aunt didn't know that I had already lost my virginity but my grandmother did. She just sensed it and she would tell my aunt. Every time they would ask me I would say no I hadn't yet.

Although this guy was very nice and respectful, I was just looking for something to not be with him. I guess in all honesty I just wasn't attracted to him. Somehow at that age I just couldn't get past that. This was someone that was about five years older than me. We stopped seeing each other and then the real story began. About a few months later someone came to visit my aunt. This time it was his middle brother. This was my first time seeing this person as he didn't come along with his mom and his two brothers when they first visited my aunt. Once again, I didn't really pay him mind; I was just minding my business. When he went home, my aunt and I had a discussion and I found out that he liked me. I was told some sad stories about him which made me feel some form of connection or pity for him. I was attracted to him, but I knew that nothing could happen between us because he was the first guy's brother. He later expressed his feelings and emotions for me and fed me similar stories that I was told about his life and his relationships with his brothers and mom. He asked me out, but I refused due to obvious reasons that he was The oldest guy's brother. I even told him that I dated his brother but he insisted. I brought it to my aunt's attention. She agreed that he was a nice and handsome young man but did not say much about me possibly dating him. He was very consistent and adamant about being with me. I told him in order for me and him to have anything going on I will have to ask his brother first. I called the older brother and told him that his brother asked me out and if it was okay with him to date him. He was shocked and started laughing which threw

Rebekah Acquah

me off-guard, but he gave me permission, so I felt that now it was okay. This was about to be one of the worst decisions of my life.

This new relationship was bitter from the very beginning. I remember one week where he broke up with me five times. He would insult me and wouldn't trust me. I found myself trying to convince him every day that I was a good girlfriend. He was very jealous and would accuse me of cheating. Things became stable for a bit. I drove my aunt's old car without her permission about forty minutes away to visit him. He introduced me to some of his friends, whom I believe were from his church. I felt that this person really liked me and this was going somewhere good. He had this sort of control over me; I didn't want to lose him. Then my second sexual encounter happened. I had no idea what I was doing or why but all I can remember was crying every single time. I didn't like it, there was no emotion tied to it, and I didn't know what I was doing. Being eighteen at the time didn't mean that I had the knowledge of what to do. It was just something to please him, not me, because I felt no pleasure at all. In the times where I didn't want to do it and I told him no, I still felt like I had to. He would say things that made me feel like that was the only option. I had the love of my aunt and my cousins but I guess that feeling the love of a man was much better. As much as I felt something wasn't right and as much as I was emotionally disconnected, I would still lay there as he penetrated me. Well, we ended up breaking up. Although my self-esteem and confidence were very low at the time, one thing I did know was that a man was not to put his hands on a woman. And one day he had the slightest of intentions to do so. That's when I realized the rage and anger that lingered in me. That night after getting the slightest hit from him I ran into the kitchen, grabbed a knife and headed back to the room and asked, "Did you just hit me?"

I could see the fright and surprised look on his face, He couldn't speak, yet managed to say my name.

76

"Gloria"

"I said did you just hit me?" He tried coming towards me, and he grabbed my hand that held the knife.

"Gloria, please I didn't hit you."

"So what did you do then?"

The next thing I knew he ran out the room door. as I ran behind him with the knife, he managed to go back into the room and locked the door with me on the outside of it.

"I will call the police," he said.

"Oh really, that will be good," I replied, "so you can go to jail for hitting me and I'll tell them it's self-defense so I grabbed the closest weapon I could."

I opened the door with the knife while saying, "No man ever will put their hands on me and go free. Now did you just hit me?"

He said, "I'm sorry Gloria, I'm sorry, it was a mistake."

As I watched him, visibly afraid, my rage slowly disappeared. He grabbed my hands once more trying to pull the knife down. When I pulled away the knife I left a dime-sized cut in his palm.

"Sorry, that was a mistake, but seriously never put your hands on a woman!"

It was a crazy night, but that's not why we broke up. I later found out that he was cheating on me by telling another female that I was his cousin and telling me that she was his cousin.

At this point of my life, at age eighteen, I was about to graduate from high school. I was completely drained with all the other things that were going on in my life, I decided to stay to myself. But I guess the Universe, my decision-making skills or my heart had not had enough, and thus it led me to my third encounter. The house phone rang over and over for about three days, and when it was finally picked up on the other line it was the same brother's mother. She spoke to my aunt that day asking her to come to a wedding with her. Now over the years my aunt and I had grown closer, and she saw me as her big daughter. She was the mother figure in my life. She asked me to come with her to the wedding and I agreed because we were always the spotlight at any event we attended. Although she didn't go out too much, she had a classy side, she was very confident and for that I am so grateful. A couple days before the wedding, she started feeling pain in her legs so she wasn't able to make it. Since she had already promised her friend, she asked me if I could still go. I asked if her older son was going to be there, and she said maybe. I was hoping that he wasn't so I was kind of hesitant to go. But because I had already promised my aunt, I went anyway. I went and dressed beautifully. The whole time I sat with their mom. I honestly don't think she knew about her sons and I, or if she did she really played it off well. When the wedding was almost over I saw him, the oldest brother. We spoke once or twice. He was with another girl that night but it didn't really bother me. The party was almost over and it was getting late. I decided to leave, but before I could, there stood before me my third encounter. I was almost out the door when he interrupted me:

"Excuse me, excuse me! Do you mind taking a picture with me please?" he asked.

I was kind of shocked so I replied, "I'm sorry, I'm on my way home and it's getting late."

"I promise it's going to be really quick, just one picture please," he said.

"Ay why not."

I took the picture and went to my car. I was getting closer to my car. He followed me and we began to chat. We talked about school and God and life. Those were the three most important things to me, especially school and God. I was hooked and interested but I thought nothing of it; I was only interested in being friends. But soon I realized in this world that being friends with a pretty girl was not possible, at least not as often as I would like it to be. He asked for my number and I didn't give it; instead I gave my social network name. We slowly but gradually became connected. He introduced me to his roommates and his cousin, and then it began. He was very nice, but everyone is nice within the first six months, right? The red flags began when he lied to me and told me that he didn't have a daughter. I was already in a bit deep when I finally got the truth out of him. All I wanted was the truth, and at this point I didn't really care whether he had a child or not. Once he said he loved God and was in school doing his masters, I was already in love, or so I thought. We talked about marriage, and once again I thought this was my husband. We prayed together, I cooked, and we would do things that normal couples or grown-ups do in relationships, including sex. The only difference is that every time I cried and AGAIN I didn't know why. I knew what was wrong because I wasn't actually married but I placed in my head that if he's going to be my husband anyway then it was right. Things began to change slowly. One day he told me that because his daughter's mother was Muslim he had to go to Africa and marry her in order to keep his daughter as his child. He told me that the wedding and the marriage was not real and that it was just for that purpose. For a second or honestly more than a second I believed him, yet something just wasn't right. At that period of my life I began to love myself; I wasn't fully there yet, but it was something. He tried to convince me, he even asked his cousin to talk to me and to let me know that he and I would still end up getting married. But he still didn't make sense as I was not about to be a second wife. Yet, something just was keeping me there with him. Something was allowing me to believe everything. I even helped him pay for the flight to Africa and the wedding and to purchase a gift for his daughter in Africa. He went and got married and came back to the United States. It didn't hit me until I saw the photos of the wedding on Facebook. That's when my beliefs and the Christian views and my conscience wasn't allowing me to live or ignore what was in front of me. They tried to convince me it wasn't real, and I remember with tears in my eyes saying to his cousin, "I can't do this; it's not right. No matter what, he is married. I can't look at this and say it's not a real marriage."

There were so many more obstacles that happened in that relationship within only six months. I found myself trying so hard to convince myself to stay because I had already given myself to this person and wanted him to be the last, but when the praying together stopped and I was left alone on my knees, I couldn't do it anymore. This all happened within the first year of me entering college.

I was now nineteen years old. Things were about to change. After that situation somehow looking back now I will say it's because of God, the oldest brother came back as a friend - or so I thought. I remember him coming one day to visit me at school and the humility just fell upon me as we were crossing the bridge at my school. I got on my knees and asked him to forgive me. He wasn't sure for what, so I told him for me hurting him and dating his brother, that I was wrong and whether with his permission or not I was wrong and I am so very sorry. He forgave me and picked me up off my knees saying it's okay. I felt some kind of release of freedom. I felt less heavy. He will come and visit me more often now and soon I figured out the reason behind the visits. This may not have been his intention yet by his actions the loudness of his behaviors spoke volumes. He one day came over to visit and I ended up going to his place because I had never been there, or maybe I was just naive. From one conversation to another, it suddenly led to the room. Kissing was all I wanted to do but I put myself in this situation, as he tried and tried to force something else but I just wouldn't allow it. Suddenly, with a strong force and a push across his shoulders, I ran out and left in anger, confusion and tears. I thanked God that nothing happened. I pretended that everything was okay and I just needed to get over everything. So I still remained friends with him, but we didn't talk for a while. When he called I would answer and talk to him like friends, normal people. Which brings me to my fourth and final encounter, which was right around the corner.

This one was different, and led me to a life of self-growth, self-love, self-appreciation, self-confidence, and helped me begin my journey of abstinence. From the age of nineteen where my third encounter ended to the age of twenty-one were some of the best times of my life. I was focused on school, my life as a Christian and my relationship with God. My self-esteem was higher than most. I felt as though my life was finally coming into a place where I was finally in control and my only focus was education. I wasn't looking for a relationship with anyone. I already had my four best friends, my relationship with my aunt was going well, my relationship with my dad was content, and I felt good. God was in my life and I felt great. I was also very aware, so I thought, of not allowing myself to make similar mistakes as before. Life is a learning process and I did not see this next phase coming.

February 14, 2013 was when I had prayed to God and told Him that I was ready to love Him completely and that I understood in His word that it was okay to be single and that singleness was a good thing because it gave more room for my relationship with God to become stronger. I even pondered on the idea of becoming a nun. I accepted my new life of singleness as a growing young woman. It felt so good after that prayer, knowing that I was not worried about guys or feeling the need to be completed by a man. My focus would be on school and God only. Then February 16, 2013 a friend of mine asked me if I have somebody in my life. I told her no but I wasn't looking and I was okay. She said okay, but someone is interested in you. I told her it's okay, because honestly, I was not looking right at the time and I was okay with being single. She told me I should just give him a try.

"You don't have to be with him. I promise you he's just like you; he's like the male version of you. He loves school and loves God and is very honest and goofy. In fact, he's in Bible study right now and I told him that I will ask you if you're okay with him sending you a message on Facebook."

I said, "Sure, he can send me a message but honestly I don't think this is going to go anywhere."

She continued to tell me a little bit more about him. Later that day after his Bible study he wrote to me on Facebook. This time it "seemed" very different. We clicked immediately. He made me laugh. It was as if I had known him for years. It felt good to have a good conversation with someone. He lived in another state so I didn't think it was going to go anywhere, which was a pattern that I had fallen into subconsciously. We continued to talk every day after that. She was right; he did seem like the male version of me. He even ended up speaking with my aunt and she automatically told me that he is my husband. I laughed at the fact that he had just one conversation with her and she already thought that he was my husband. Since she is very wise, some things she says actually come true, so that thought stayed in my mind for a little bit. Once again, I was totally focused on God and school and I equated that to be my husband. We spoke for about three months, and then he came to visit me at school. Well, several times, it was nice, and I began to fall in love. After a few months, he came to visit and that's when it happened. I told him that I didn't want to; I told him I was waiting for marriage. I told him that this is not what I wanted to be; this is not me. I tried to convince him that sex outside of marriage was not what I wanted. Yet somehow, I guess it all just went from one ear to the other, and with hormones and everything raging, I was unheard and even I couldn't hear nor believe myself either, so it happened. Something felt strange and different. I still cried, but felt something different. I still knew it was wrong but still it was different. It was different because I felt that he was genuine, because I felt that he actually loved me. Thinking that maybe my aunt could've been right and that he was actually my husband, I became comfortable because we became comfortable with each other. I still cried, but I became comfortable and gradually I believed the concept that God had approved because this was my husband. We and I dated for a while. A year went by. He met my family. I met his family and I was introduced to his three-year old daughter. This actually felt real. It felt as though everything was coming into place with my education, my relationship with God and having my own family. Although we had arguments and problems it was not over the top, I could tell that we loved each other. People around us saw that what we had was special. He became so many things to me that I was missing before, or at least I felt so. We began to talk about marriage and moving in together. We reached the point where I was given a promise ring, and then he bought a ring to ask for my hand in marriage. We were so close to moving in together, but I was fighting so hard to not lose my relationship with God, which was the one thing that kept me sane. It was that one thing that kept me from reliving my past. I couldn't allow myself to be ungrateful, so I stood my ground and said that we are not married, I couldn't move in with him just yet. I didn't want to be like everyone else I thought to myself, although I was that way already. I wanted to uphold my reputation of a good person that follows the "rules." I felt like I was different ; I felt there was something about my life that was just not like anyone else. I felt I was chosen for something but didn't know what. If my conscience didn't allow it, I fought it. We ended up breaking up because of a different situation. When we did, the realization that convincing myself to do things that I was against was not going to lead me to my true happiness took its course. I realized that every time I partake in sexual acts and then forgive myself, I would become unhappy. I know it's not right and that's why I always cry. That's this feeling that I get ...

it is not a feeling of happiness or joy. The feeling I get is from something deep down within my soul that tells me, "This is not you." In that moment I realized that my relationship with God was most important than my relationships with these men, and who I will get involved with will be determined by the promises they make and my own free will. Honestly that's when I knew that I was also more important. My happiness in having a free conscience, loving myself, and my confidence, was more important. I made the decision to become abstinent. I knew it was going to be hard, especially when the guy came back. I was drawn to him; he was like my drug that I was addicted to because of the many years, the intimacy, the closeness, the connection, our ups and downs, the goals and dreams we planned together, and I got used to him. After I told him that I was now abstinent, he laughed continuously and said that it's impossible for him to be. I also asked if we can actually try to grow some kind of friendship instead of just the intense attraction. He told me that he could never be friends with me because he's still in love with me. I couldn't understand. How can you love someone without friendship and why couldn't he want to wait for me now because it was clear that we broke up? All of those promises of marriage and my reasoning to partake in intercourse with him was based on those promises. Because of that breakup it was not guaranteed.

I ended up in the Emergency Room due to a panic attack from our breakup and from feeling drained, lost and empty. I no longer had my family. The connection to his daughter and losing it hurt me the most. I felt as though I had lost so much. Nothing's really guaranteed until it happens, I said to myself. I learned from all of my mistakes; it took me four times. The last one was the hardest hit for me to begin realizing my worth, my value and the importance of God in my life. The signs were there. The warning voice was low, but it was there and I ignored it. It took me being placed into a terrible situation to wake up, pay attention and to STOP! Like I said, I'm just like you. I'm not perfect, but with my mistakes I am now abstinent one year and counting. Sometimes it takes tragedy in our lives to put us back on the right track for a greater purpose and light up the unquenchable happiness within. I see it as a call from God to return to who we truly are. I have dated since then but I make sure I let the person know at the beginning removing any miscommunication . I took time off to date myself. I took myself out on dates, I said kind words to myself. My conscience is my best friend now. If something does not make me happy, I say so and then I don't do it. Realizing your worth is very important. And I now understand that if a man truly wants you after you've made it clear to him where you stand, he will not say anything or try to persuade you to do something that is against your desires and your beliefs. There are men out there who are capable of authentic love. But first we must love ourselves to be able to receive or give that authentic love. Although sex or making love brings a level of intimacy, it is only a reward for the connection that was built prior. Because there are many different forms of intimacy, and from my experience to where I am now, the best intimacy is the love that I have for myself. This self-love allows me to give and experience true love with another. Similar in some ways, yet different, my experience got me to realize that I do have control, and that my spirit and my body are very important. Your experience may be different, yet the lesson to be learned here is that we all must love ourselves, our bodies and our spirits and understand that we need to have control and we are very important. Our conscience lets us know this. I ignored my conscience on many levels, and the tears came in all four encounters. I ignored it, but I now understand that making the same mistake will only lead to our downfall. So please take this experience of mine in understanding that you have control, you are important, your body is important, your soul is important, and you are worth true and authentic love from another. You deserve true authentic love from yourself.

Chapter 12 - Forgiveness

I was on a great path, and things were falling into place a little at a time. My relationship with God had increased even more. Yet, there was still a void; something that was stopping me from "complete freedom:" a freedom that would allow me to put my best foot forward; a freedom that brings forth a heart to love, and an experience to bring peace. Something was wrong somewhere. I thought I had already blocked this out and had forgotten all about it. I believed that my thoughts and mind towards this topic was already concealed and put to rest. But deep down inside I knew that the emptiness within me could only be filled through the act of "FORGIVENESS." Not just forgiveness for others that I felt hurt me, but forgiveness for myself for wrongfully hurting others who only wanted to help me, and for wrongfully hurting myself and not loving me.

For me to forgive myself I had to fill the void. This void came from my father. He was the man I loved so much without really knowing much about him. I wished he did not abandon my mother and me. He was the man I had hoped would've told me more behind his reasons for leaving when I asked him at age sixteen. He was the man I blamed for my mistake of losing my virginity, the man I blamed for not being there to guide me about not dating older guys. I would have wanted to have a fatherly figure because he was already that father, the man I didn't want to love and wished I hated at times but couldn't find it in my heart to stay away from wanting him in my life. I knew he was a wonderful father, but just not to me. He was the man I hoped to prove me wrong about him letting me go. I knew I had to forgive my father because my entire life surrounded the first decision he made before I was born. I realize that despite all the improvements in my life I still wanted to be "daddy's girl." I still felt unhappy. I was searching for love in all the wrong places all my life and all I needed was my father's love.

Although I had told myself that God is my Father and his love was the only love I needed, somehow, I would still cry on Father's Day, or I still felt a void. I believe that God chooses our parents for a reason. I also believe that our stories are thought out for a purpose, so it was not a mistake when he created my dad for me. It was all in his plan. I have learned so much from the absence of my father. I have also learned a lot from his presence. I called my father and told him that I forgave him, and the reasons why I was hurt. Moments later I texted him these words:

"Hi Daddy, I've been a little distant. I've been this way because I've felt disappointed. I've felt a little hurt and the only way I felt I could handle these feelings was to distance myself from the core of it all. But it's more hurtful to me and more damaging than it is helping. I deserve love and I truly believe that God needs an empty heart and a clear heart, mind, and spirit to pour that love into my life. So I am letting go of all the daddy issues I had up until this very moment. I am letting go of all the missed birthdays, empty promises, broken hearts, father-daughter conversations, the missed protection, and everything that I may have needed from you growing up. Although I am letting go of these things, I will not let go of you. Your absence has somehow blessed my life and thus made me the woman that I am today: strong, positive, determined, caring, loving, forgiving, promising, and God-fearing. I was set aside by God. I am blessed with the people that have surrounded my life in your absence. I am doing this for myself. After I send this to you I know there will be a freedom that I've never experienced because of my daddy issues that weighed me down. I didn't want to admit this to myself; I didn't want to admit that your absence in my life was affecting me. I didn't want to give you that victory over my life so I blocked it all and now I'm opening the door and letting go. I'm unblocking it all. I proclaim that I am free, empty, cleansed, and purified (like a virgin). I am ready for that authentic love that God is about to replenish over me. I thank you Daddy, I love you Daddy, and I will always love you. I will always be there/here for you; do not EVER hesitate to ask me for help with open arms. I am your daughter and I will gladly give what I can, and however God allows me to thank you. Love you always.

We talked for about an hour, and His response gave me peace within. He mentioned how sorry he was, and that he loved me. He wants my happiness and if I decide that I would be happiest with him out of my life completely, he would respect my decision. But, he is here and ready to turn the page and start fresh. He wants to be in my life more and connect with me. He wants us to communicate, although he is in another state. If I need anything, he told me I should just ask. That's all he wants is what makes me happy because it is my life.

I appreciated my father's words and whether our relationship was going to develop from there on was not my immediate concern. My heaviness was uplifted at that moment. I had forgiven my father and finally was able to forgive myself. Our relationship grew from there; we talked often and freely. I became comfortable with him and he was real. He started sending me fifty dollars a month and put me on his phone plan. I did not care about the amount; what I saw was him putting in effort and that meant a lot to me. I tried not to think about all the things he was doing for my half-sisters; instead the focus was on our relationship. My efforts to continue going to school and proving him wrong for letting me go had changed. I was more focused on going to school and being a wonderful young woman for myself and my family as a whole. I wanted to make my aunt Olu, my mother and myself proud. So even though I was struggling financially in college, I did my best to not ask my father for money. I wanted him to continue to be a great father to my sisters as he and I built our relationship. I didn't want to make him feel as though I only wanted money from him. I wanted him to understand that all I wanted and needed was his attention and love. I still understood that he had another family that he was dedicated to. One thing that I knew for sure was that I loved my father and he loved me. Finally, he started seeing me for me and not what he thought I was by what he heard, nor what he thought I would become. The void that I felt that was preventing my growth was slowly diminishing.

This is why forgiveness is so important. It allows the peace that passes all understanding to be immersed in your spirit. There was nothing weighing me down. I did not allow negative feelings to overtake my life or my circumstances. Once forgiveness is fully achieved, then freedom, peace and joy will follow along eventually.

Chapter 13 - Breaking Away (From Christ)

I still read my Bible and I still prayed, but didn't feel like enduring the stares from others at church who were probably wondering where the rest of her family was, because most people knew my Aunt Musu and were familiar with the Thelman family. I was pretty quiet and stayed to myself when I went to church. I enjoyed the singing and the Word. Then one day I just didn't feel right anymore. I would only go to church because of the music, but once the music stopped and the pastor began to preach the Word I couldn't understand what he was saying anymore. I couldn't grasp what he meant. I felt that I was only going to church because of the music, and I didn't want that. I didn't like it, even at that time I can truly say I was still hungry for more of God, and because I wasn't receiving what I was hungry for at that age, I stopped going. When Sunday came I would feel restless and tired. I got comfortable with staying home, saying a prayer or two and call it a day. My aunt and most of my family at the time didn't really put much effort in attending church either and they were content with staying home on Sundays.

For two years I was distant from the bosom of Christ. During those two years everything became difficult; suicidal thoughts got worse, and then I had mood swings. There were still a few good times. During those two years I began volunteering at a geriatric center across the street from my high school and I loved it. Within almost two years I gained some form of self-esteem by participating in Miss National American. My aunt was really supportive, and she did all that she could do to try and make me happy. My aunt tried to help me to understand that she loved me just as she loved her kids. For me it was very difficult to accept. I felt like I reminded her of the mistreatment that she received when she was younger from our family. I did not know how to be what she deserved and needed. I didn't yet know how to be me or who "Gloria" was. I lost interest in God and in myself for a moment.

Chapter 14 - Finding My Way Back (To Christ) - College Days

It was Move-In Day to the college dorms. I was ecstatic to be on my own at college. I felt a change coming. I had been away from church for a while now, and I felt that this was a new beginning for me. I wasn't sure how to start, so for the first six months I joined my school's Campus Crusade. This was like a club where Christians or kids who just want to know about God would come together, pray and read the Bible. I went often but then still something was missing. I don't know what it was; I just knew that something else was missing. I needed more; I was hungrier for God's Word. I would cry every time I prayed. There was so much pain, frustration and hurt that I just wanted to be emptied out. Everywhere I went on campus and whomever I talked to somehow the topic of God came up in the conversation and I found myself talking on and on about God. I made a few attempts to visit one of my friends' church (who was in the campus Crusade Club) but that didn't go as planned.

One day, randomly, I was hanging around with an upperclassman who was my good friend and she introduced me to one of her friends, Lamar. Once again, we started talking about regular stuff but somehow God came in the midst and it wasn't too long when Lamar invited me to his church. At this time, I had no vehicle, and if I was going to take the bus I was never going to make it to any place of worship. Lamar suggested that someone in the church would pick me up. I couldn't believe how easy it was. I wasn't even expecting anything special on that day. This invitation pleased me and the bosom of God. He wanted more from me. The kindness and service by one individual made an impact in my journey. This is why I believe that each of us has a role to play in each other's life. We may not know nor understand which role we are playing, because I believe that Lamar didn't know that by inviting me to the place of worship, it would have a significant impact on my life. My friend who introduced me to Lamar – she played a new role in my story. This is why I am not the author. We are not the authors of our lives because it was not my decision to place them in it. I did not know I would meet my friend or Lamar. I did not know that entering Living Peace International Church would bring me back again in to the blessings of God. All I wanted to do was to be near to God once more. On the first Sunday I was picked up by Patricia Harrison, who later became Auntie Pat. She was the first impression besides Lamar that would make the reconnection with God divine. As I entered the service I gained a family of supporters; I gained a sense of belonging. There was this feeling that overtook me that made me feel as though God was opening his arms and saying "Welcome My child; I've been waiting for your return."

This experience resonates with life in general. For those who may feel that the Universe at times may be punishing us, we will feel that it's hard to pick ourselves up or find a place of belonging in this world. All we need to do is to make a conscious decision. We need to know what we want and ask for it. The Universe (if one does not believe in God), bring individuals or things into our lives that will direct us into what we ask for. If we set our minds on a specific piece of our lives that we feel is fading away into dangerous places, and we don't want to be in that position or that place, then simply ask for the help and do your part in the process. Let's focus on where we want to be, and it will take us to that new place. The Universe will welcome us back, saying "Welcome my child; I have been waiting for your return." We already have everything that we need; it's only for us to reach it and grasp it. We sometimes forget that we were once at peace, and we sometimes forget that we were once in a place of no worries. We sometimes forget that there was a time where we loved ourselves; joy and happiness were once there. It is possible to return to that place, and this experience of reconnecting with God by him placing people in my life to help me reconnect with Him taught me this lesson, that He was already there. He was there with open arms and returning back to Him changed my life. It was the beginning of what was to happen further along my life. Even with all the obstacles, struggles, tribulations and backsliding along the way, my return was significant. It took consistency of continuously asking for guidance and claiming the peace that was already mine.

As you go through life, instead of fighting the Universe or fighting against the joy that you deserve, the peace that you deserve, the happiness that you deserve, take it as it is already yours. You do not need to run after those things, it is already within you. Joy, Peace and Happiness are not to be chased but rather to be released from your inner being.

In moments like these, we recognize our fire, because if we are active for something that we feel we deserve and already have, there is probably something within that is lit up to experience what you believe you deserve. You deserve a sense of Joy, a sense of Happiness and a sense of Peace. You deserve to understand and know your purpose. If your heart is bitter, or your mind has been contaminated with lots of distractions and unhealthy or unworthy things, remind yourself of your worth and remove unhealthy things from your life. You deserve better. Give way for that unquenchable fire to be lit up. The burning bush may have already been lit from your birth, but it is recognizing it that allows it to glow and shine. We recognize, then we act, then we grab what belongs to us, which is that inevitable Joy. I recognize that my burning bush was that I had to return to God. You may already have something in your life that gives you ultimate inner peace and you may feel that it is far from your reach. Maybe it's you and maybe its self-love;

maybe it's forgiveness! Whatever it is, be still, recognize it, claim it, grasp it, and listen for the voice to say, "Welcome back! I have been waiting for your return."

Chapter 15 - Homeless Impact at Newark Penn

Ministry in Newark Penn Station. changed my perspective on what it meant to have faith. From as young as I can remember, there was always a connection between me and those who did not have much. Here is a journal entry on my outreach to the homeless in Newark Penn Station.

God Gives Let's Give Project

Today was a very good day. It was more than good; it was a blessing. Today was the first day of the beginning of my goal and dream of helping the homeless and being there for them, even if it's just to give an ear to their stories about life, or maybe to give some change here and there, or even to give them snacks or something to eat. I know I can't do much right now, but just putting a smile on someone's face makes me happy. What God has taught me in life is to give, even if it's your last. Well if you feel it's your last, because you are a child of God it's never your last. You have a Father who provides what you need, and protects you even if you don't notice His protection. He loves you when you feel there's no more love in this world.

Today marked my first visit to Newark Penn Station. I visited my third family (others call them the homeless). They are my family because they give me hope. They make me feel more appreciated, and they help my trust to grow, because they trust strangers for so many years to donate to them, no matter how many rejections and negativity they've experienced. If a person can still get up and continue to ask those same people for help and money every day of their life for years, I see that as courage. My third family has courage and faith. I met Jackie, Elliot, Vance and a few others, but I remember Elliot and Jackie most because I actually conversed with them. Our conversation was the most pleasurable, special and blessed moment of my day. Jackie is a fifty year old married woman who lost her legs. Now I met her sitting in her wheel cheer under a metal roof/covering. it was so cold outside today but she was all bundled up which made me happy inside that at least she was warm. Our conversation automatically started and if I'm not mistaken it lasted for about twenty to thirty minutes. Jackie told me she was homeless for nine years since 2005 the year she lost her legs and, guess what? Her son died because he was shot in a drive-by shooting. He saved two people and didn't even know he got shot until he was suffering from internal bleeding and died (tears). Jackie never went to college but she has two daughters; one graduated with a Bachelor's degree and the other went to college but only stayed three to four days and dropped out because she did not think college was for her. Jackie has family members as well. Now some people may ask why was she homeless for nine years, and honestly I asked Jackie the same question. When she told me that she and her husband had been married for twenty-nine years, I thought that was a very wonderful thing.

I said to her, "Wow, that's wonderful and a blessing that you've been married that long, but I'm curious. Please if I may ask why you are homeless then?"

She said, "At the time we weren't divorced, but we were separated and my daughter couldn't take care of me because she was in college." She then pointed across the street showing me where she used to sleep. She explained how she would sit all day outside by a pole, which she showed me. I learned a lot about Jackie, and I was very interested in her life story. It seemed as though all she wanted was to talk to somebody. As our conversation continued, tears rested in my eyes; I tried to turn my face a bit so that Jackie wouldn't see the tears. I learned that almost everyone died in threes, from Jackie's friends to her family members. She found her brother dead at home on the floor due to brain damage from alcohol. Her mother and father passed away as well.

Then I asked her how she lost her legs. My curiosity and concern led to a very sad truth after she said these words, "From being homeless for so long, in these streets, my legs was no good anymore." She continued, "This is what people don't understand, do you think I want to have no legs? I didn't want to be homeless but they don't realize what we go through and until a person becomes homeless and experiences what we experience it will be hard for them to know the struggle and truth. I thank God because I know it wasn't my time to go. That's why even though I was homeless for nine years, I am still alive today and things are getting better. They're not all good yet, but I am blessed because I have an apartment now and I'm not homeless anymore."

Jackie was absolutely right and that is exactly what I told her. She was even concerned about me, whether she was holding me up from going somewhere or not. Not knowing that she was the reason why I was there, I simply told her, "No, I'm okay. I love talking to you and you're not holding me up."

She asked me where I came from, and I told her I live on campus at a University. This is when her daughters came up in the conversation. Her oldest daughter is twenty-four years old, so by doing the math I realized that her daughter was fifteen when Jackie became homeless and lost her son. During our conversation people walked by. Some stared at me like I was crazy, and a few stopped and gave Jackie a dollar in her cup. A very generous man even gave her $13. God bless his soul.

A young female passing by stopped to ask Jackie, "If anybody could help you with one thing what would you want?" Jackie replied: "My legs."

The young lady was shocked and said to Jackie, "I can't give you your legs but what else would you want?" Jackie paused and said, "Nothing then, because I have an apartment now." I then jumped in and said she was homeless for nine years. This fact shocked the young lady again and she simply said, "Wow; nine years."

Her friend was waiting for her so she told Jackie, "I'll talk to you again, hopefully," Jackie replied, "You'll see me here again at this same spot tomorrow." Their brief two-minute conversation just affirmed to me what I always thought about my third family (homeless people). They are human beings just like us and are not selfish or greedy. They do not want all your money or want to be on drugs. They are just like you and me, and even better because, like Jackie, they have hearts and all they want is one thing, their life back. It could be their family back, their home back, their job back that they lost because of the economy, their honor back and as in Jackie's case their legs back. Jackie was very honest throughout our conversation I could tell it was all honesty. She kept bringing up God and faith and blessings, and even if she made the simplest mistake where she didn't recall a situation in her life correctly, she said, "Sorry, Lord" and corrected herself. After the conversation with the young lady while I was thinking how wonderful this woman Jackie was, a man came to Jackie and gave her a pack of cigarettes (which wasn't filled). I must admit it was very cold outside, and I was freezing a bit so that made me ask Jackie, "How long is the person you're waiting for going to be before they come?" She told me that was her husband; he's the one that was waiting for her and that he's very protective of her and shy. I waved to him. I still was thinking why they were in this cold if they had an apartment. Now that I think about it, being homeless for nine years at the same spot day to day month and years going by, a person will certainly find it hard to not come back to that same spot after gaining a home. Perhaps Jackie has gotten so used to being homeless and sitting in that spot that every day she felt that's where her true home is. Perhaps that became more of a home than a building, so it will take time to stop coming back or getting used to not being homeless. She told me how she still reminisces on her son's death and still misses him. Of course a mother will never forget her child, especially by the manner in which she lost her baby boy. I reassured Jackie to stay warm and I hoped that she would be leaving soon. Then she asked for my number and we exchanged phone numbers, in hopes that maybe when I call her it would be the call that would make her day better. She tried to give me a handshake but I simply gave her a hug. She said it was nice talking to me and that was what she needed. She thought I was a sweet girl and hopefully I would call her. We said our goodbyes and I was off on my way back inside of Newark Penn Train Station.

This is where I met my next family member, Elliot, who introduced me to his brother Vance. Walking into Newark Station, there weren't many people earlier, but then I guess around that time (not knowing exactly how long I've been at the station) there were more people (family, homeless) than before, so I looked for a spot to sit and someone to talk to. My goal was to talk to and connect with women, so I sat next to a family (homeless) woman and said, "Hi ." She didn't really respond much, even when I asked for her name. But her expression looked like she was one of my family members who suffered from mental illness. On my right there was a man standing up eating Ramen noodles (the cup looked like it had been kept for days, or even weeks) but his look brought peace because he was happy and enjoyed his meal. I said hi and he replied hi. That's how I met Elliot. We began our conversation. Elliot is a fifty-four year old man (which I never would've guessed because he looked ten years younger) who had two brothers. He was the middle child. He lived in Newark and went to an institute and graduated. He comes to Newark Penn every day and has an eighty-year-old mother who is a Registered Nurse (RN). He said she comes to the station to help the homeless at times. I told Elliot about my school and he asked me what was I studying, and I told him Clinical Psychology which he figured that I liked people and I affirmed that to him. We even started talking about each other's families, and he asked about my parents. That's when he found out that I was African and that's when I found out he was good at math because he guessed the age I came to America based on what I told him. Elliot is a very nice man, and during our conversation his brother came and I was introduced to Vance, who made me laugh. He said, "My name is Vance, as in dance, lance, ..." It was funny how he said it. It reminds me of how Jackie made me laugh when she was telling the story about her legs and the man who gave her a very tall prosthetic leg and it made her taller than every man, so she had to take it off to feel better. Vance was also nice and I felt comfortable with both of them. I don't understand why people are scared to talk to people who are homeless if they've never made an attempt to hurt them. They are homeless, but they are people. Elliot asked me if I could spare two dollars and I told him the truth on why I couldn't grant his request. He did not stop talking to me nor did he get upset; he simply said, "Okay, I understand. God bless you for even talking to me." He asked me if I come to the station every week and I explained to him I used to stop there on my way home, but I'd stopped, and I had just started again. I planned to return every Wednesday, though. He seemed happy to hear that news. I was so into the conversation that I almost forgot that I had a train to catch. I quickly looked at the time and told Elliot I had to go but would return next week, he shook my hand and said, "See you next week, and keep warm."

I told him to keep warm tonight as well and said goodbye to him and his brother Vance. They now know me as Gloria.

So yes I had a WONDERFUL, HAPPY, AND VERY BLESSED DAY on 2/12/2013. I learned a lot and I appreciated a lot as well. Today is the first day for a lifetime of memories with my third family, aka the homeless. I can't wait for next week. God bless the homeless ...

God Gives, Let's Give. "God Gives, Let's Give" is the name that has been revealed through a dream to me to help God's people, those in need of a friend, a sister or a helper, and those in poverty. Today I understood the reasons behind my experiences so far.

I later went through more experiences with the homeless. Not only through speaking with them but through my own personal homelessness for two weeks. I had been taking summer classes for two years without an issue with the university paying for my room and board during the summer. But this summer, 2014, was different. Room and board was no longer covered during the summer due to funding being cut, and there was no way I was going to not take my free summer classes that will enable me to graduate on time or even early. I knew I couldn't travel every day for an hour on the train to class. I would've been late, plus the expense on my aunt to ask her for money when I didn't have all the time, even though she wouldn't have minded: I still believed there was another way. I began the summer by asking my friend, who was a Residential Assistant to sleep over, but there's a limited amount of time that visitors are allow to sleep over. I slept in my car for the remaining weeks of my summer classes. I did not mention anything to anyone, not even my aunt. My routine for the two and a half weeks was to wake up at 5am when it's a bit dark, change into my clothes for the day, use a bottle of water and the travel size toothpaste I got from CVS store and brush my teeth. Then without showering I put deodorant on, wash my face and wait for sunlight to come out to head to the library as I waited for class. After class I would either meet up with my friend, hang out, eat something and tell her I would see her tomorrow. When she asked if I was going home I answered, "Something like that." I would head to my car or to the library to charge my phone to 100% because they closed late. In my car I would have my phone in hand while I prayed with the gospel music on, and head to the back seat to sleep soundly. I got used to the routine and fear was far away from me. I still made my trips to visit my homeless family at Newark Penn. I felt protected and covered by the hands of God every day in my car. After classes ended, I returned home and received an "A" for the summer. That summer I gained so much appreciation and love for those who have no home or a place to go for education. I didn't know that my experience for the two and a half weeks was to understand my purpose that God would later reveal to me in fullness in my life.

Chapter 16 - My Impeccability and Life Purpose (A Letter to MySelf)

Dear Gloria Mansa,

My name is Gloria Mansa. I was born in Monrovia Liberia, located in West Africa. I have seven brothers and sisters and I am the oldest girl by one day but the only child from my mom and dad. I have never lived with either of my parents for more than six years. During the time of my birth, my country had just ended a civil war and times was very hard on my mother who was abandoned by my father. During her pregnancy with me she fell on her belly after seeing a war plane flying overhead which led to me being born with my left leg slightly handicapped. Meanwhile in the African culture they always try to find natural remedy for everything, so my aunt who helped my mother out during her pregnancy pulled my leg every day until it became straight. Due to after-war hardship, my father's sister, who was in the United States at the time, sent for some family members on a refugee program. Since I was her brother's daughter, my name was included. Although it was very hard for my mother to let go of her only child, she made the tough decision for my future and told me I was going to America. At the age of seven I had no idea what was going on, I remember leaving my mom and crying so much, and that was the last time I saw my mother in person.

Coming to the United States was very different from what I was used to. I had a very heavy Liberian accent. My cousin threw up on the plane because the American style food was different from a normal African dish. I was placed back two grades because of my heavy accent (language barrier). At that time, I still didn't know who my father was; I just knew his family. Staying with his sister was a bit difficult and a lot went on during my preteen years from nine to thirteen. There were problems at home, which led to me running away between four to six times. Depression affected me, as well as loneliness and suicidal thoughts. At the age of twelve I was molested by an uncle, but what never left my spirit and heart is the love of God. I would pray every night before bed and sleep with my Bible beside me. I was constantly in and out of homes, because my dad's sister was constantly working. She was a tough parent and very hard working.

Praying and writing poems finally paid off. God answered my prayer, but it took me running away for the last time for a miracle to happen. That miracle is what brought me to where I am today in my life. I ran away one last time because the mistreatment was too much for me. I cried every night, and that helped me realize that I couldn't take it anymore. Honestly, running away at twelve was one of the best decisions of my life.

Looking back on the decisions in my life, I can say that at the very beginning I was thrown around by the adults in my life; they had control over me. I was living their life, and as I grew up, like most of us, I began to find myself. There were and still are times when people in my family try to place spells on me with their words. For example, the words that affected me the most was when I was told by my caregiver at the time that, "You have nobody, your father doesn't want you and you will be useless in life if you don't take time." My father, whom I still had not met, and lived he in America as well, heard from his sister that I was a bad child, so he agreed to send me back to Africa. Those words lived with me until a few years ago.

I victimized myself as depressed, lonely and a nobody. Those words took root in my mind until I decided one day to uproot those planted roots. I decided not to water those negative seeds anymore but instead I planted new seeds; seeds of empowerment, seeds of self-love, seeds of living for the good and seeds of love. The first step towards changing myself was when I noticed I was being self-critical and I allowed others to treat me as I treated myself. The day that I made an effort to soften that self-critical voice, a positive me came forth. I also received great help from God when he sent my guardian angel to give me a second chance at the American dream. My aunt Olu, who I currently live with, went against everyone in my family and took me in her home rather than giving up on me and sending me back to Africa. While with her I was still in my depression and in a suicidal state of mind, but because she also came from a rough past, she stood by me and supported me. She helped me gain my confidence back. One way was by me participating in a NATIONAL AMERICAN MISS PAGEANT, which helped me tremendously. My aunt Olu helped me find not only my speaking voice within but a singing voice I never knew I had. My new spell was a positive one. My aunt's words were uplifting. She told me I had a beautiful voice and that I am a beautiful girl. That became the new spell and because it was a positive spell, I lived with it until it became my identity. My aunt Olu has been ostracized by the family because of her kindness towards helping not only me, but others who have no home and no one to lean on. She is a single mom who is struggling every day to survive for her children, yet she gives like she has the world. She stood by me since I was in my mother's womb, and now that I am about to graduate from college a semester early, against all the odds, I truly believe she deserves the Greatest Supporter award. This woman has been my aunt, my second mother, my friend, my father figure and my up-lifter. She has helped strengthen my faith in God and to never give up on myself and life. Her words, "Keep on going girl, God has it under control. The rejected stone shall be the cornerstone; just keep praying." She does not understand the impact she has had in my life. I am beginning graduate school ; I am moving away from my aunt Olu to continue my education in Clinical Psychology. I cannot leave without giving her a rose of gratitude.

My confidence grew so much that now I think I have the confidence level of above average. Participating in the pageant also led me to do volunteer work, and since then I've been working at the place where I volunteered when I was in the pageant. I've been singing and doing activities with the elderly. I have done a little modeling, and I've sung at different events. I still write poetry and I love the homeless.

At the age of sixteen I met my father, and I had to forgive him because God always forgives me for all my wrong deeds. My life has been a roller coaster ride and this is only a brief summary. If I go into greater detail it might become a novel, but I am grateful for every single obstacle and difficult time and most importantly my aunt Olu, because it made me who I am today: the bubbly, open minded, happy, God fearing and now educated young woman who has so much greatness ahead. Because of my upbringing and my past, the seven spiritual laws of success strongly play a role in my life today.

My outlook on life and the way to live has changed tremendously in an optimistic way. I can honestly look myself in the mirror and say that I exemplify true potential because I know who I am. I perceive myself as exuberant, open-minded, respectful, and an extrovert. I am someone who loves being a servant of God, and a gifted communicator with senior citizens and young children. I am very motivated in everything that I do. I am someone who can be counted on. I have goals and I plan to reach every one of those goals. I am living the dream because I am still alive. I believe in loving your neighbor as yourself and though at times I do it subconsciously, I try my best to not judge others for who they are. I am someone who believes that anything and everything is possible. For me the sky's not the limit, it is only the beginning, so I aim higher each day.

I once had so much guilt weighing me down as a child and a teenager, which put a huge hindrance on my creativity and enjoyment of life. Now I have a new agreement to live each day as a blessing and enjoy it in the way I know how within my spirit. Wishing people bad is not in my heart. When I am angry I agree to try my very best to have positive thoughts. I've learned in life that people will always try to push you to your limits whether intentionally or unintentionally; it is up to me as an individual to practice how to meditate on positivity because even if they do you wrong if you do them wrong back, the process of karma will continue and another wrong will be done to you. One of my unique ways of giving back is by working with the elderly and asking God to protect the homeless and the world. I aspire to become a Clinical Psychologist to give to those who are shut down and belittled by society; and to those who are homeless, uneducated, mentally ill, etc.

These things may make it seem as though I am close to perfect, but that is the opposite. I truly believe I do more good than bad, and think more positively than the average young adult. I am impeccable, and the positive words that I speak upon my life have a huge impact on me. Meanwhile, God is still working on me and I am still working on myself. I make a lot of mistakes, but to value my pure potential and live with others is to know myself and how I can improve the world and my inner spirit. This is what I try to do as I learn from my mistakes. I will follow these four agreements: to love myself, to love others, to not take things personally, to stop making assumptions, and to do my very best. My presence in this world is to simply live as freely as I can and as I do this I am able to give the world an impeccable being. As an impeccable being I live in my now; I do not allow the past to affect me, and I do not worry about the future things because the Universe (God) takes care of those worries and things of the future. As I acknowledge where I am now I bring physical, mental, and emotional peace to myself.

I now know who I am as a person and once God gives me the basic needs of my life, I am at peace with myself. I live in my now; I take control of the time. Time stands still and moves when I am ready for it to move. Even though its physical hands are still moving around, my mental and psychological time is at peace. I am no longer rushed by the clock as those who depend on it so much. Living in my NOW gives me complete control and peace. I can love those around me right now, love who I am right now and do what I need to do in this very moment freely.

The agreements that I have decided to make in my life carries power. This breaks the majority of fears that I have. For example, because of past experience I had the fear to love and I had to learn that it was because I feared loving myself completely and did not feel that I could ever be loved at that particular time. But this agreement that I made in my life has been life-changing. My fear to do things, to love, to receive, to express myself have all been cast into the past and now I can love others because I love myself. I can receive because I want to continue the universal art of giving and receiving. I can express myself freely because I have chosen and agreed to be free. I am impeccable, great, beautiful, and loved.

Chapter 17 - The Agreement

This agreement was written on 12/5/2014 for the purpose of increasing my happiness and personal freedom. I am responsible for creating my personal dream of heaven on earth, and it begins with the power of my word.

Reflection of Impeccability

I am amazing. I can make myself the happiest person in the room even if everything seems to be otherwise. I am kind hearted; I am accepting of new changes. I am that young lady that will go up to a stranger who is crying and say, "You are beautiful" just to put a smile on their face for a moment. I have the ability to forgive without holding a grudge. I see life as something just passing by, and instead of stressing over simple things I find a positive outlook to not stress. Yes, I at times take things lightly that others may take as a serious problem, but it is my way of calming them down and seeing positivity.

I am a person who gets upset when pushed too far and comes back with words that may hurt momentarily. Meanwhile, I am that same person that comes back after a minute or so to apologize, whether wrong or right. I possess a genuine smile, and a genuine heart. I yearn for those that I love to understand how much love and care is in my soul for them. At times I want to be open so that my love and care for others will be shown to those who doubt. I am a great writer but a not so great editor.

I love the Lord Jesus and feel the need to say it everywhere if allowed.

I honestly do not like restrictions and rules. I love to talk and love to listen and help others. Sometimes I confuse myself by thinking too deeply into everything people say. I like the art of knowing and not just having an idea tossing around in my mind.

I am unique, I love simply saying hi to everyone and I do not think it should be a problem. I am a confident individual. I take pride in having my own way of doing things and having a form of independence. I am someone who expresses themselves more through writing and songs than spoken words. As Dr. Phil once said, "When you're asked, 'Who are you?' what is your answer?" "I'm a student." "I'm a psychology major." "I live in Florida." Often the answer is not who I am, but what I do, what my social status is, or how I see my function in life. For a while I could not answer the question "Who am I?" because I did not know. Even though I may not be fully aware of the entirety of which I am, right now I can honestly say that I am closer to me than before.

There is another level of existence that is the real, true, and genuine substance of who I am. The authentic self is the me that can be found at my absolute core. It is the part of me not defined by my job, function or role. It is the composite of all my skills, talents and wisdom. It is all of the things that are uniquely mine and need expression, rather than what I believe I am supposed to be and do. God created a perfect spirit in me; I am happy, I am me.

I agree and choose to love myself and treat myself with respect, dignity and care. I will look up to me and encourage myself each day that I am the best. I choose to not be a victim nor a judge because that will take away my happiness. I will do my best at everything I do. I choose to be impeccable with my words, my actions, and myself. I will live in my now and not let the burden of the past and future overpower my present. I promise to speak with integrity and choose my words carefully. I intend to use my words to encourage, uplift, love and share the art of happiness with others. I will repeat these actions until the habit is strongly established and no longer requires my attention. These actions and agreements that I choose today will become my identity. The symbol of my commitment to this agreement is my "word."

I agree to stop blaming everything and everyone else for my lack of freedom. By blaming everything that goes wrong on others, it will only bring pain and dissatisfaction. I must learn to take care of myself first and accept that I only have the power to change things for the better. Taking full responsibility and being aware of my faults is the only way that I am able to fix the issue and re-dream a better dream, with actions included. I once lived in this world in constraint and was stopping myself from being free, spiritually, and emotionally. I am replacing that lack of freedom with the agreement of having the freedom to love and not be afraid to be loved as well. I have freedom from judging and accepting being judged. As long as I am doing my best, I agree to be happy. I am agreeing to keep that inner child within me and live in the present. It is understood that I have responsibilities and at times I need to put on a serious face, but as I place that tough and serious face on, I agree to keep a happy spirit, a childlike spirit that would encourage me to see the light and joy in every responsible thing I come across to do. I vow to live my life how I have learned to live it in these past few years; to please myself and not others. By pleasing myself I would please others because there is joy and happiness in my heart and inner spirit for everyone I come across. Pleasing myself and agreeing to the four agreements, life is much easier and contains less stress. I agree to make my own heaven on earth, not having to die before enjoying heaven because God is always present and the kingdom of heaven is everywhere. It's just a matter of accepting this truth.

My dream of the past is over, and though I have already started a new uplifting dream, I will continue to stay within this dream and improve upon it in a positive aspect. The parasites of this world will not take away my newfound peace and me finding myself and pure potentiality. Being impeccable with my word, not taking things personally, not making assumptions and always doing my best are things I am going to work on. I know these agreements will take a while to truly come to life within me, but I am not giving up until I see more improvements in myself love. I believe the agreement that I may have a harder time achieving is not taking things personally. I have to learn to not attach emotion to everything people say, especially things that family and loved ones may say that will bring negativity. This agreement shall remain.

Chapter 18 - Purposeful Alignment

There you have it: my story. It is not the full story because I am still growing, making mistakes and learning each day of my life. But it is the story that brought me to where I am today, that changed my mindset on how I view life, people and myself. It is the story that allowed me to recognize who the Author really is. It is the story that is most significant in forming my purpose, because it consists of the beginning, in the middle, and as I lived towards the end which is not really the actual end, I am grateful for what has already been written in my life. In the first stages when the author began imprinting my story with which I was conceived and how I was conceived, I thought I may have been a mistake. I was born into a family that was against the relationship of my parents, and I was born in times when the country was in turmoil. I was born when my mother was in tears and sorrow, during the time when Liberia was lifeless, in a country of people who had given up in hopes of a better future. I was born with no proper medical attention; it is only by the grace of God that one who is born in such conditions or one who is placed in such conditions can survive. That was no mistake; that was done on purpose. That is where I now hope to return after experiencing privilege in the country on the opposite side of the world from where I was born, in a country that is thriving, in a country of hope and confidence. There is still a fire within me that burns to return to where I was born. I was born into my purpose.

My story, my life, as you have read, has been filled with turmoil, obstacles, tensions, frustrations, depression, suicidal thoughts, anger, misery, temptations, mistakes, setbacks, loneliness, tears, negativity, discouragements, betrayals, hopelessness, and everything that is set before an individual to break down and never rise again. But it is within those difficult situations and negativity that helped me to be as strong and optimistic as I am today. Those challenges were made not to deter me from my purpose in life, but rather to prepare me for purposeful living. My experiences align with my purpose for which I was created to contribute to the Earth. Have you ever wondered what your experiences brought you to? When we take a minute to rest and figure this out, we become closer in understanding our purpose for being born.

We are all designed with unique passions and gifts, things in life that bring us pure joy. Yet, passion is not enough; it is a part of the process of exploring and finding "the work," and "the purpose." The work and purpose is for service to others.

My life today is a gift and a privilege from God. I recognized that I owe it to those children who were once like me, and to those people who are also going through situations like I did. I owe it to those individuals who felt emotions as I did, to them, to myself and to my Author who is God, to do something. Therefore my purpose in life, from the moment I entered this world, is to simply give. Give my time, give my knowledge, give hope, give encouragement, give my heart, give my energy, give my friendship, and give what I have been given throughout my journey. I've been given a second chance at living a purposeful life and acknowledging that I was placed on this earth for a purpose. So, to begin in my works of giving, I have been directed to begin with and the place where I was born to educate those young children who have not yet understood their purpose. I want to impact children who have been in poverty from the day they were born and who are not a mistake on this earth but do not have anyone in their lives that they can look to for hope. I want to reach those children who are being punished for things they have no control over, for things that their ancestors did, or for things that generations prior to theirs had committed. I do not, no I cannot sit around knowing that God has placed in my heart my purpose to give back that privilege of knowledge in education, that privilege of knowledge and hope and that strength that He has placed within me how to thrive in life and be happy. I cannot sit and watch the children in need the most be in the bondage of mental poverty, spiritual poverty, emotional poverty and physical poverty. I understand how being in the bondage of mental, physical, emotional spiritual poverty feels like and what it can do to you.

Through building schools, mental health clinics, homeless shelters and outreach programs in Liberia, giving them a place where they can come and thrive in all the sectors of their lives and express themselves freely is my mission. It is God's vision and the Author's purpose of my life to give.

Because the experiences of my story, I now understand what it feels like to have a house but not feel at home. My encounters with those who are homeless taught me how important the gift of time and a simple smile means more than what money can buy. It is through the homeless individuals that I truly felt what it meant to have a relationship with God. Each homeless individual, no matter their circumstances, has been in the cold for years, and have been kicked off benches, without food or clothes, having their legs amputated because of the cold, being looked at by strangers as dirt and nothing more: those encounters were very vital to my life. Why? Because although they went through those times in their lives, there was still hope in their eyes. They still believed that there was a God and for those who I met that didn't believe in God, I saw in them strength in the mustard seed of faith. This is one reason why God placed on my heart those who are in poverty; it's my purpose to give. There's a time for everything, and there is a season for everything - and that season, I believe, is for the purpose of living. Living to give to the homeless and to those who are in mental, spiritual, physical and emotional poverty has come. I strongly believe that the first steps, the second steps and the third steps have been completed. We all go through the steps in our lives which is why it's very important to sit down, think and feel what your life truly means. As we all know, in order to get gold or diamonds, we have to go through the dirt, in the mud and through the fire to become valuable, and not all gold or every diamond is created at the same time. There is a waiting process for each item of gold to be formed. And as one is formed, the crafter who places that gold into the fire understands how to create the next batch of gold. The knowledge sticks, and just as diamond that diamond that knowledge is shared with someone they know every so often from one person, knowing where that diamond is, it becomes known to those individuals, and they go and dig for another diamond. So just as life is, once you recognize how precious you are to this world, it is your duty to place that same gem within someone else, thus allowing the individual, that friend, that stranger to be just as priceless as you are. They need to recognize that whatever they are going through, they have to go through that fire that you went through to be able to recognize that they are gold or diamonds. That same refining process happens to all of God's children, and it happens to all important people of this world.

For those who are meant to live that purposeful life, it only takes recognizing that purpose. It takes you sharing your story for someone else to understand the reasons behind their struggles, their disappointments, their obstacles, their lonely days, their negativity, their fire and their dirt. I hope that by me sharing and expressing and telling of the fire that God had written in my life, it will encourage someone to understand their importance on this earth.

I encourage you to organize your purpose because it is already there; it just takes recognizing. It took me twenty-two years to first recognize it, and now I am looking forward to my next encounters that are coming before me to fulfill my purpose. At times I've wondered how I can change or impact an entire nation alone? I question every vision and dreams and ideas that God gave me; I didn't feel worthy enough. With no financial stability, how am I supposed to give and do the things and fulfill the purpose that God wanted me to fulfill, the one in which I am called and created to do? I must be crazy to even think of such a large task. Well, that is exactly what I am - "crazy" - and that's a reason to keep believing and working towards this purpose. If you are too comfortable in what you are currently doing, if it does not scare you at times, and if it does not spark something different in you, a passion each day, then you are not completely living the purposeful life destined for you, the one that is required of you.

Chapter 19 - Secrets to OUR Happiness ☺

Towards the end of writing this book I began to reminisce on its purpose. The book was intended to be an inspiration. Recently I searched in my heart and my spirit to identify who I've been inspired by and how inspiration can change lives for the better. There have been many women in my life that I've been inspired by, and four in particular, through their words, have become inspirational and uplifting in my life. Because of these women my life changed. My aunt Olu, my mother Beatrice, Oprah Winfrey and Dr. Maya Angelou. The four women are two I know personally and two I've only heard their stories and their words from afar. All four women have inspired me in similar ways through their strength, their stories, and their willpower to carry on despite what they've been through. Their courage, optimism, and perseverance - and more specifically the one thing that exudes excellence in their will to touch others and keep going is their faith in God. Hearing the stories of these women and being able to be personally a part of two of them (my aunt and mother) and how they have changed and impacted my perspective on life, I can't help but think about the purpose that a story holds. The power of what one story, once it is released out in the world can do to a generation. Lately I've been listening to Dr. Maya Angelo and Oprah Winfrey. I've been listening to their messages, their stories, their memories and their life lessons. I've been seeing how they have impacted and inspired so many generations, women and lives. How they've gave hope and led others out of depression and internal life issues. My aunt, an inspirational woman, allowed me to have faith in God and in myself. I remember during the time of my green card season I had lost a lot of my documents and I became weary and disappointed and discouraged that things weren't going to go right. I started losing hope that whatever the naysayers around us were saying was going to happen, because everything was not working out. Then my aunt said to me one day, "Where is your faith?" In my stubbornness I tried to act as though I had faith, so I said to her, "I'm not losing faith in God." She asked again, "Where is your faith? Why are you worrying? You can't do this; only God can. If God brought you this far where is your faith?" And every time since then, when I come up to face another obstacle in my life, I make sure that my faith in God is there. It is through faith in God's will in my life, manifested through these powerful women of inspiration, led me to where I am today and is leading me to where I am going. What I think about during these times of reflection is the next generation and the many generations to come around the globe. I have been privileged to have inspiring women in my life even though they may not have noticed that they were inspiring to me, but I can't help but think of who will be there to inspire and to encourage the next young woman. Who will be the next Oprah Winfrey, Maya Angelo, Olu or Beatrice? There is a fire within me that yearns to touch every dry leaf in my path, because these fires I believe have been passed on from inspiring women. This fire is like the burning bush that Moses saw and heard the voice of God, and that burning bush, that fire cannot be quenched by water. Every dry leaf that is touched, their fire burns to touch another. I was once a dry leaf, and it took inspiring women to touch me to light my unquenchable fire, so I will not be living a purposeful life if I keep whatever that has been ingrained in my soul, in my spirit, and my being, to myself. If I keep the lights from shining into others that have been passed on to me that is selfishness. And even though the burning fire cannot be quenched by water, by not paying attention to the fire within it will slowly die away and become lost. I think of the Universe in different groups, meaning that God gives all of his children talents and gifts, and these gifts and talents are different and that's how you find some people can read and a fire is lit in someone else, and others can sing and that hits a spot in someone else. Then, there are speakers and nurses and doctors that just by one touch or one word that they say changes a life or saves a life. What makes it different is that with each talent or gift there are others who have similar talents and gifts. It's like a project in a classroom; the classroom is filled with different students of every shade, size and talent. You are placed in groups, and in each group everyone has a similar talent or gift as the others, but within the group there are different ages which represents different generations, so each generation passes on a sense of wisdom to the next generation in that group. That inspiration continues, and for the entire class to be a successful class, each group has a role to play. Their assignment must be a success for a successful class overall. What makes it a success is what each generation teaches the next generation. If it's positive it grows; if it's negative then what has been taught dies away. Going back to the four women who inspired me positively, that needs to grow. If I withhold what I have been taught and do not pass it onto the next generation, I believe that I am hindering the development of a successful class overall. Just as writers have inspired other writers to spread a similar message on to other writers, they impact generations to impact other people who have other talents, just like singers have impacted other singers to share a message to impact those who don't have a singing voice, but they have other talents.

We all have talents that work together or should work together for the good of empowering the world, the Universe, to have a successful humane life that God has promised us. With every talent that we have, deciding to use those talents is where free will and selflessness comes in. Do we only benefit ourselves, or do we benefit each other? For those of us who decide to be selfish instead of selfless to continue spreading the good, we place a hindrance on the successfulness of the overall human resources. Therefore, as I look at my life story because I am not the author of my life, I realize that the Author has placed many talents and gifts within me. I believe that I have the choice to be in different groups in this Universe but where my purpose is fully defined is through education, which is why the people who have inspired me also found purpose in educating others. That is my assignment, my group. Now education does not only mean in the classroom, and that's what makes each of us who have similar talents and assignments still have a sense of uniqueness in our gifts because "talents" and "gifts" are different. We may all have similar talents but different gifts. For example, there's a lot of singers but each one has a different gift to touch different people. My purpose is to educate, but my gift will educate in a way that is different from those who inspired me. I have been privileged to have come this far, to have been led to this path of where I have obtained my master's degree. Through this course of my life, I believe that my talent and my gift will fulfill the purpose of why I am on this earth. Because of the story that has been written by the Almighty Author, He has used inspiring women and inspiring outcomes in inspiring situations to manifest his glory into inspiring the next generation. Through my struggles with poverty and mental illness, I am inspired to continue the work of leading many out of poverty through education. Poverty can lead to a mental illness/disorder and mental poverty is a mental disease. Education deals with the mind which eliminates some mental illnesses. I say "some" because for those with severe mental diseases/disorders, classroom education solves or eliminates only partial mental illness, but not all. The one that remains is more of an uncontrollable mentality, when something else takes over the mind, and how to control that is where a therapeutic procedure, which may also include medication, takes place. Mental illness (uncontrolled) is when a person has been through the process of mental poverty and or is already born with a mental delay. Being through the mental poverty phase and now experiencing severity of that, which is the actual depression, schizophrenia, anxiety, social disorders, delusional disorders, hoarding, etc. (This mentality can be solved through therapy and if necessary, medication included.) The goal is to use education to solve the first stage that prevents the second stage. But those who are already within the second stage when they are discovered, need to find ways to help them gain control of their mental illness and then return them to the first stage where education can be used, therefore making progress to better their lives in both the controlled and uncontrolled mentality. Separating the two mental disorders/diseases and attacking both the controlled and the uncontrolled types changes lives. Mental Poverty: (Controlled) is when someone does not think of themselves as important, capable, deserving, thus is unaware of things happening around them. One that has been placed in a mentality of unimportance which leads to mental depression, anxieties, hopelessness, hearing voices to give up, and fear to talk to people. This mental poverty can be solved through education. Many of us are suffering and going through mental poverty, where mental poverty is most severe in third world countries. As Maya Angelou once said "just do right," so I'll add on and say, "doing right for people in need is doing right for my spirit."

So if you ask me where I am today in my life, my next stage is to not forget the words of my aunt, "Where is your faith?" to "Just Do Right" "Give with Purpose" and live by the steps of the one who is writing me an inspiring story for the next generation ... God.

Until next time, remember I am just like you, and as you have gotten to know more about me, be inspired to do and be what you want to be. Do not allow your past to determine the great future that is before you. Tell your story and be an inspiration. Let's pass on the burning fire that is unquenchable. You are not alone, let's reveal the secrets to our happiness!!

Chapter 20 - What's Your Story? Our Unquenchable

Happiness definitely continues and certainly does Gloria's. Her story continues.

Now it's your turn. Remember when I mentioned that I'm just like you? Well, it's your turn to share your story.

How has Gloria's story made you view life differently? How has her story impacted you?

This story is not just about Gloria; it's about you and me, which equals the US. I want to hear your story, the World needs to hear your story, because your story is unique. Your journey it's special. Your voice is beautiful, and you have virtuous gifts and talents that can change someone's life. This is your chapter! This is your chapter where you will begin to tell your story. Pour it all out on these next pages. Come on, you can do it. It's time for you to change lives. Grab a pen or a pencil, write on these blank pages, take pictures of what you've written and forward it to (rebekahacquah@gmail.com), with your permission your story will be told!! You already have the pages right in front of you. Let your fire, your burning bush, ignite another dry leaf. BE IMPECCABLE!!

You are UNQUENCHABLE

#ourstory #BurningBushUnquenchable #Unquenchable

CHAPTER 21 - BLANK PAGES FOR YOU

REFERENCES

Chapter Two

1 WGBH Educational Foundation. "Liberia -No More War." PBS, Public Broadcasting Service, May 2005, www.pbs.org/frontlineworld/ stories/liberia/facts.html

Chapter Six

Aratani, Y., & Cooper, J. L. (2015). The Effects of Runaway-Homeless Episodes on High School Dropout. Youth & Society, 47(2), 173–198. http://doi.org/10.1177/0044118X12456406.

https://www.ncjrs.gov/pdffiles1/ojjdp/196469.pdf

https://www.1800runaway.org/wp-content/uploads/2015/05/NRS-Longitudinal-study-full-report.pdf

www.ingramcontent.com/pod-product-compliance
Lightning Source LLC
Chambersburg PA
CBHW030914100125
20156CB00009B/87